The Great Contraction

1929-1933

The
Great
Contraction

1929-1933

MILTON FRIEDMAN
ANNA JACOBSON SCHWARTZ

A STUDY BY THE
NATIONAL BUREAU OF ECONOMIC RESEARCH, NEW YORK

PUBLISHED BY
PRINCETON UNIVERSITY PRESS
PRINCETON, NEW JERSEY

8-7-90

First PRINCETON PAPERBACK Edition 1965

Fifth Printing, 1973

This is a reprint of Chapter 7 of the authors' *A Monetary History of the United States, 1867-1960* (Princeton University Press for National Bureau of Economic Research, 1963). It includes certain other materials from that publication.

Printed in the United States of America by
Princeton University Press, Princeton, New Jersey

RELATION OF THE DIRECTORS
TO THE WORK AND PUBLICATIONS
OF THE NATIONAL BUREAU OF ECONOMIC RESEARCH

1. The object of the National Bureau of Economic Research is to ascertain and to present to the public important economic facts and their interpretation in a scientific and impartial manner. The Board of Directors is charged with the responsibility of ensuring that the work of the National Bureau is carried on in strict conformity with this object.

2. To this end the Board of Directors shall appoint one or more Directors of Research.

3. The Director or Directors of Research shall submit to the members of the Board, or to its Executive Committee, for their formal adoption, all specific proposals concerning researches to be instituted.

4. No report shall be published until the Director or Directors of Research shall have submitted to the Board a summary drawing attention to the character of the data and their utilization in the report, the nature and treatment of the problems involved, the main conclusions, and such other information as in their opinion would serve to determine the suitability of the report for publication in accordance with the principles of the National Bureau.

5. A copy of any manuscript proposed for publication shall also be submitted to each member of the Board. For each manuscript to be so submitted a special committee shall be appointed by the President, or at his designation by the Executive Director, consisting of three Directors selected as nearly as may be one from each general division of the Board. The names of the special manuscript committee shall be stated to each Director when the summary and report described in paragraph (4) are sent to him. It shall be the duty of each member of the committee to read the manuscript. If each member of the special committee signifies his approval within thirty days, the manuscript may be published. If each member of the special committee has not signified his approval within thirty days of the transmittal of the report and manuscript, the Director of Research shall then notify each member of the Board, requesting approval or disapproval of publication, and thirty additional days shall be granted for this purpose. The manuscript shall then not be published unless at least a majority of the entire Board and a two-thirds majority of those members of the Board who shall have voted on the proposal within the time fixed for the receipt of votes on the publication proposed shall have approved.

6. No manuscript may be published, though approved by each member of the special committee, until forty-five days have elapsed from the transmittal of the summary and report. The interval is allowed for the receipt of any memorandum of dissent or reservation, together with a brief statement of his reasons, that any member may wish to express; and such memorandum of dissent or reservation shall be published with the manuscript if he so desires. Publication does not, however, imply that each member of the Board has read the manuscript, or that either members of the Board in general, or of the special committee, have passed upon its validity in every detail.

7. A copy of this resolution shall, unless otherwise determined by the Board, be printed in each copy of every National Bureau book.

(Resolution adopted October 25, 1926,
as revised February 6, 1933, and February 24, 1941)

Contents

Experience in controversies such as these brings out the impossibility of learning anything from facts till they are examined and interpreted by reason; and teaches that the most reckless and treacherous of all theorists is he who professes to let facts and figures speak for themselves, who keeps in the background the part he has played, perhaps unconsciously, in selecting and grouping them, and in suggesting the argument post hoc ergo propter hoc.

ALFRED MARSHALL

Preface

THE collapse of the United States banking system during the course of the business contraction from 1929 to 1933 and the failure of monetary policy to stem the contraction had a profound influence on men's ideas. In the worlds of scholarship and policy alike, these events led to the view that monetary phenomena primarily reflect other economic forces and that money plays at most a minor independent role in economic affairs. The inference was drawn that policy designed to prevent or moderate economic fluctuations must assign major emphasis to governmental fiscal action and direct intervention.

A paradoxical result followed from the influence of the monetary events of 1929-33 in shaping men's ideas about money. The view that money plays only a minor role in economic affairs led, for several decades, to the virtual neglect of the study of monetary phenomena, including the monetary events of 1929-33. Only recently has there been a renewal of interest in this field of study. Accordingly, we were led to devote a lengthy chapter to the climactic four-year period of the Great Contraction in our book, *A Monetary History of the United States, 1867-1960*. Indeed, one-sixth of the book is devoted to just these four of the ninety-four years our analytical narrative covers.

We concluded that the wrong inference had been drawn from the experience of those four years, that the experience was a tragic testimonial to the importance of monetary forces, rather than evidence of their unimportance. The drastic decline in the quantity of money during those years and the occurrence of a banking panic of unprecedented severity were not the inevitable consequence of other economic changes. They did not reflect the absence of power on the part of the Federal Reserve System to prevent them. Throughout the contraction, the System had ample powers to cut short the tragic process of monetary deflation and banking collapse. Had it used those powers effectively in late 1930 or even in early or mid-1931, the successive liquidity crises that in retrospect are the distinctive feature of the contraction could almost certainly have been prevented and the stock of money kept from declining or, indeed, increased to any desired extent. Such action would have eased the severity of the contraction and very likely would have brought it to an end at a much earlier date.

Moreover, the policies required to prevent the decline in the quantity of money and to ease the banking difficulties did not involve radical innovations. They involved measures of a kind the System had taken in earlier years, of a kind explicitly contemplated by the founders of the System to meet precisely the kind of banking crisis that developed in late 1930 and persisted thereafter. They involved measures that were actually proposed and very likely would have been adopted under a slightly different bureaucratic structure or distribution of power, or even if the men in power had had somewhat different personalities. Until late 1931—and we believe not even then—alternative policies did not involve any conflict with the maintenance of the gold standard.

Robert M. Tayler, an undergraduate at Earlham College, who read our book, suggested to us the desirability of reprinting as a paperback the chapter in *A Monetary History* on "The Great Contraction, 1929-33," so that it would be readily available as supplementary reading for college courses that deal with that episode. We are grateful to him for the suggestion and to Princeton University Press for acting on it.

Though "The Great Contraction" is reasonably self-contained and can be understood without reading the chapters that precede or follow it in *A Monetary History*, as a convenience to readers of this paperback reprint, we have included a glossary of terms and full source notes to charts.

One regrettable omission here is acknowledgment of the numerous and heavy debts we incurred to many individuals and institutions for assistance in the course of writing *A Monetary History*. For a partial list, we must refer the reader to the preface of the book.

Comments by Albert J. Hettinger, Jr., a director of the National Bureau, that appear at the end of *A Monetary History* are reprinted here, since they deal mainly with this chapter.

M. F.

A. J. S.

The Great Contraction

1929-1933

CHART 16
Money Stock, Income, Prices, and Velocity, in Reference Cycle Expansions and Contractions, 1914–33

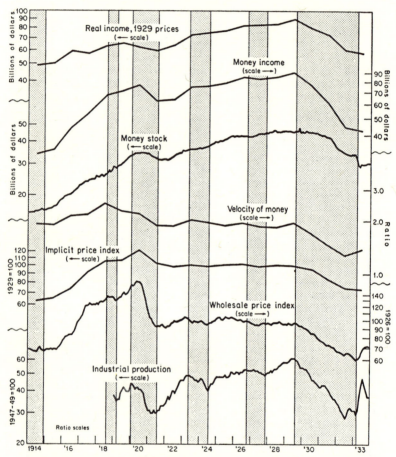

NOTE: Shaded areas represent business contractions; unshaded areas, business expansions.
SOURCE: Industrial production, seasonally adjusted, from *Industrial Production, 1959 Revision,* Board of Governors of the Federal Reserve System, 1960, p. S-151 (manufacturing and mining production only). Other data, same as for Chart 62.

The Great Contraction, 1929–33

THE CONTRACTION from 1929 to 1933 was by far the most severe business-cycle contraction during the near-century of U.S. history we cover and it may well have been the most severe in the whole of U.S. history. Though sharper and more prolonged in the United States than in most other countries, it was worldwide in scope and ranks as the most severe and widely diffused international contraction of modern times. U.S. net national product in current prices fell by more than one-half from 1929 to 1933; net national product in constant prices, by more than one-third; implicit prices, by more than one-quarter; and monthly wholesale prices, by more than one-third.

The antecedents of the contraction have no parallel in the more than fifty years covered by our monthly data. As noted in the preceding chapter, no other contraction before or since has been preceded by such a long period over which the money stock failed to rise. Monetary behavior during the contraction itself is even more striking. From the cyclical peak in August 1929 to the cyclical trough in March 1933, the stock of money fell by over a third. This is more than triple the largest preceding declines recorded in our series, the 9 per cent declines from 1875 to 1879 and from 1920 to 1921. More than one-fifth of the commercial banks in the United States holding nearly one-tenth of the volume of deposits at the beginning of the contraction suspended operations because of financial difficulties. Voluntary liquidations, mergers, and consolidations added to the toll, so that the number of commercial banks fell by well over one-third. The contraction was capped by banking holidays in many states in early 1933 and by a nationwide banking holiday that extended from Monday, March 6, until Monday, March 13, and closed not only all commercial banks but also the Federal Reserve Banks. There was no precedent in U.S. history of a concerted closing of all banks for so extended a period over the entire country.

To find anything in our history remotely comparable to the monetary collapse from 1929 to 1933, one must go back nearly a century to the contraction of 1839 to 1843. That contraction, too, occurred during a period of worldwide crisis, which intensified the domestic monetary uncertainty already unleashed by the political battle over the Second Bank of the United States, the failure to renew its charter, and the speculative activities of the successor bank under state charter. After the lapsing of the Bank's federal charter, domestic monetary uncertainty was further heightened by the successive measures adopted by the government—distribution of the surplus, the Specie Circular, and establishment of an Independent Treasury in 1840 and its dissolution the next year. In 1839–43, as in 1929–33, a substantial fraction of the banks went out of business—about a quarter in the earlier and over a third in the later contraction—and the stock of money fell by about one-third.[1]

The 1929–33 contraction had far-reaching effects in many directions, not least on monetary institutions and academic and popular thinking about the role of monetary factors in the economy. A number of special monetary institutions were established in the course of the contraction, notably the Reconstruction Finance Corporation and the Federal Home Loan Banks, and the powers of the Federal Reserve System were substantially modified. The contraction was shortly followed by the enactment of federal insurance of bank deposits and by further important modifications in the powers of the Federal Reserve System. It was followed also by a brief period of suspension of gold payments and then by a drastic modification of the gold standard which reduced it to a pale shadow of its former self (see Chapter 8).

The contraction shattered the long-held belief, which had been strengthened during the 1920's, that monetary forces were important elements in the cyclical process and that monetary policy was a potent instrument for promoting economic stability. Opinion shifted almost to the opposite extreme, that "money does not matter"; that it is a passive factor which chiefly reflects the effects of other forces; and that monetary policy is of extremely limited value in promoting stability. The evidence summarized in the rest of this chapter suggests that these judgments are not valid inferences from experience. The monetary collapse was not the inescapable consequence of other forces, but rather a largely independent factor which exerted a powerful influence on the course of events. The failure of the Federal Reserve System to prevent the collapse reflected not the impotence of monetary policy but rather the particular policies followed by the monetary authorities and, in smaller degree, the particular monetary arrangements in existence.

The contraction is in fact a tragic testimonial to the importance of monetary forces. True, as events unfolded, the decline in the stock of money and the near-collapse of the banking system can be regarded as a consequence of nonmonetary forces in the United States, and monetary and nonmonetary forces in the rest of the world. Everything depends on

[1] For an interesting comparison of the two contractions, see George Macesich, "Monetary Disturbances in the United States, 1834–45," unpublished Ph.D. dissertation, University of Chicago, June 1958.

how much is taken as given. For it is true also, as we shall see, that different and feasible actions by the monetary authorities could have prevented the decline in the stock of money—indeed, could have produced almost any desired increase in the money stock. The same actions would also have eased the banking difficulties appreciably. Prevention or moderation of the decline in the stock of money, let alone the substitution of monetary expansion, would have reduced the contraction's severity and almost as certainly its duration. The contraction might still have been relatively severe. But it is hardly conceivable that money income could have declined by over one-half and prices by over one-third in the course of four years if there had been no decline in the stock of money.[2]

1. *The Course of Money, Income, Prices, Velocity, and Interest Rates*

Chart 16, which covers the two decades from 1914 to 1933, shows the magnitude of the contraction in the perspective of a longer period. Money income declined by 15 per cent from 1929 to 1930, 20 per cent the next year, and 27 per cent in the next, and then by a further 5 per cent from 1932 to 1933, even though the cyclical trough is dated in March 1933. The rapid decline in prices made the declines in real income considerably smaller but, even so, real income fell by 11 per cent, 9 per cent, 18 per cent, and 3 per cent in the four successive years. These are extraordinary declines for individual years, let alone for four years in succession. All told, money income fell 53 per cent and real income 36 per cent, or at continuous annual rates of 19 per cent and 11 per cent, respectively, over the four-year period.

Already by 1931, money income was lower than it had been in any year since 1917 and, by 1933, real income was a trifle below the level it had reached in 1916, though in the interim population had grown by 23 per cent. Per capita real income in 1933 was almost the same as in the depression year of 1908, a quarter of a century earlier. Four years of contraction had temporarily erased the gains of two decades, not, of course, by erasing the advances of technology, but by idling men and machines. At the trough of the depression one person was unemployed for every three employed.

In terms of annual averages—to render the figures comparable with the annual income estimates—the money stock fell at a decidedly lower

[2] This view has been argued most cogently by Clark Warburton in a series of important papers, including: "Monetary Expansion and the Inflationary Gap," *American Economic Review,* June 1944, pp. 320, 325–326; "Monetary Theory, Full Production, and the Great Depression," *Econometrica,* Apr. 1945, pp. 124–128; "The Volume of Money and the Price Level Between the World Wars," *Journal of Political Economy,* June 1945, pp. 155–163; "Quantity and Frequency of Use of Money in the United States, 1919–45," *Journal of Political Economy,* Oct. 1946, pp. 442–450.

CHART 27
Money Stock, Currency, and Commercial Bank Deposits, Monthly, 1929–March 1933

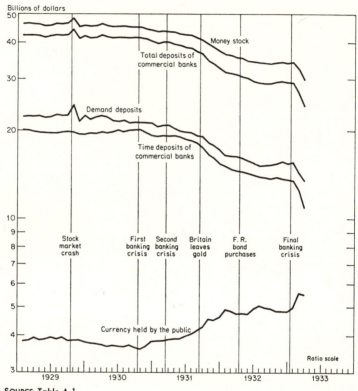

SOURCE: Table A-1.

rate than money income—by 2 per cent, 7 per cent, 17 per cent, and 12 per cent in the four years from 1929 to 1933, a total of 33 per cent, or at a continuous annual rate of 10 per cent. As a result, velocity fell by nearly one-third. As we have seen, this is the usual qualitative relation: velocity tends to rise during the expansion phase of a cycle and to fall during the contraction phase. In general, the magnitude of the movement in velocity varies directly with the magnitude of the corresponding movement in income and in money. For example, the sharp decline in velocity from 1929 to 1933 was roughly matched in the opposite direction by the sharp rise during World War I, which accompanied the rapid rise in the stock of money and in money income; and, in the same direction, by the

CHART 28

Prices, Personal Income, and Industrial Production, Monthly, 1929–March 1933

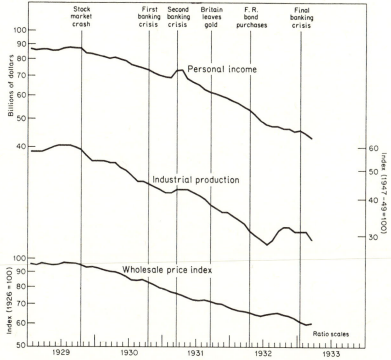

SOURCE: Industrial production, same as for Chart 16. Wholesale price index, same as for Chart 62. Personal income, *Business Cycle Indicators* (Princeton for NBER, G. H. Moore, ed., 1961), Vol. II, p. 139.

sharp fall thereafter accompanying the decline in money income and in the stock of money after 1920. On the other hand, in mild cycles, the movement of velocity is also mild.[3] In 1929–33, the decline in velocity, though decidedly larger than in most mild cycles, was not as much larger as might have been expected from the severity of the decline in income. The reason was that the accompanying bank failures greatly reduced the attractiveness of deposits as a form of holding wealth and so induced the public to hold less money relative to income than it otherwise would have held (see section 3, below). Even so, had a decline

[3] See Milton Friedman, *The Demand for Money: Some Theoretical and Empirical Results,* New York, National Bureau of Economic Research, Occasional Paper 68, 1959, p. 16.

CHART 29
Common Stock Prices, Interest Yields, and Discount Rates of
Federal Reserve Bank of New York, Monthly, 1929–March 1933

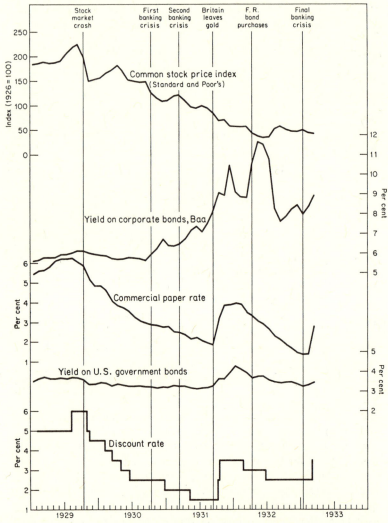

SOURCE: Common stock price index, Standard and Poor's, as published in *Common-Stock Indexes, 1871–1937* (Cowles Commission for Research in Economics, Bloomington, Ind., Principia Press, 1938), p. 67. Discount rates, *Banking and Monetary Statistics*, p. 441. Other data, same as for Chart 35.

in the stock of money been avoided, velocity also would probably have declined less and thus would have reinforced money in moderating the decline in income.

For a closer look at the course of events during these traumatic years, we shift from annual to monthly figures. Chart 27 reproduces on an expanded time scale for 1929 through March 1933 the stock of money, as plotted on Chart 16, and adds series on deposits and currency. Chart 28 reproduces the series on industrial production and wholesale prices, and adds a series on personal income. Chart 29 plots a number of interest rates—of special importance because of the crucial role played during the contraction by changes in financial markets—and also Standard and Poor's index of common stock prices and the discount rates of the Federal Reserve Bank of New York.

It is clear that the course of the contraction was far from uniform. The vertical lines mark off segments into which we have divided the period for further discussion. Although the dividing lines chosen designate monetary events—the focus of our special interest—Charts 28 and 29 demonstrate that the resulting chronology serves about equally well to demarcate distinctive behavior of the other economic magnitudes.

THE STOCK MARKET CRASH, OCTOBER 1929

The first date marked is October 1929, the month in which the bull market crashed. Though stock prices had reached their peak on September 7, when Standard and Poor's composite price index of 90 common stocks stood at 254, the decline in the following four weeks was orderly and produced no panic. In fact, after falling to 228 on October 4, the index rose to 245 on October 10. The decline thereafter degenerated into a panic on October 23. The next day, blocks of securities were dumped on the market and nearly 13 million shares were traded. On October 29, when the index fell to 162, nearly 16½ million shares were traded, compared to the daily average during September of little more than 4 million shares.[4] The stock market crash is reflected in the sharp wiggle in the money series, entirely a result of a corresponding wiggle in demand deposits, which, in turn, reflects primarily an increase in loans to brokers and dealers in securities by New York City banks in response to a drastic reduction of those loans by others.[5] The adjustment was

[4] As in pre-Federal Reserve times, J. P. Morgan and Company assumed leadership of an effort to restore an orderly market by organizing a pool of funds for lending on the call market and for purchase of securities. But the bankers' pool did not stem the tide of selling. By the second week after the crash the phase of organized support of the market was over.

[5] During the two weeks before the panic on Oct. 23, loans to brokers for the account of others by reporting member banks in New York City declined by $120 million, largely as a result of withdrawals of funds by foreigners. From then to the end of the year, those loans declined by $2,300 million, or by no less than 60

orderly, thanks largely to prompt and effective action by the New York Federal Reserve Bank in providing additional reserves to the New York banks through open market purchases (see section 2, below). In particular, the crash left no mark on currency held by the public. Its direct financial effect was confined to the stock market and did not arouse any distrust of banks by their depositors.

The stock market crash coincided with a stepping up of the rate of economic decline. During the two months from the cyclical peak in August 1929 to the crash, production, wholesale prices, and personal income fell at annual rates of 20 per cent, 7½ per cent, and 5 per cent, respectively. In the next twelve months, all three series fell at appreciably higher rates: 27 per cent, 13½ per cent, and 17 per cent, respectively. All told, by October 1930, production had fallen 26 per cent, prices, 14 per cent, and personal income, 16 per cent. The trend of the money stock changed from horizontal to mildly downward. Interest rates, generally rising until October 1929, began to fall. Even if the contraction had come to an end in late 1930 or early 1931, as it might have done in the absence of the monetary collapse that was to ensue, it would have ranked as one of the more severe contractions on record.

Partly, no doubt, the stock market crash was a symptom of the underlying forces making for a severe contraction in economic activity. But partly also, its occurrence must have helped to deepen the contraction. It changed the atmosphere within which businessmen and others were making their plans, and spread uncertainty where dazzling hopes of a new era had prevailed. It is commonly believed that it reduced the willingness of both consumers and business enterprises to spend;[6] or, more pre-

---

per cent. Loans on account of out-of-town banks fell an additional $1 billion. More comprehensive figures show a decline of roughly $4.5 billion in brokers' loans by out-of-town banks and others from Oct. 4 to Dec. 31, and a more than halving of total brokers' loans.

For the data on New York City weekly reporting member bank loans to brokers and dealers in securities, see *Banking and Monetary Statistics,* Board of Governors of the Federal Reserve System, 1943, Table 141, p. 499, and, for quarterly estimates of the total of such loans by all lenders, see *ibid.,* Table 139, p. 494. Although both tables show similar captions for the principal groups of lenders— most of whose funds were placed for them by the New York banks—except for loans by New York City banks for their own accounts, the breakdowns are not comparable. In the weekly series, "out-of-town domestic banks" include member and nonmember banks outside New York City and, to an unknown amount, customers of those banks, whereas in the comprehensive series that category is restricted to member banks outside New York City. Similarly, "others" in the weekly series cover mainly corporations and foreign banking agencies, but in the comprehensive series include also other brokers, individuals, and nonmember banks.

For loans except to brokers and dealers by New York City weekly reporting member banks, which also increased in the week after the crash, see *ibid.,* p. 174. Also see the discussion of that episode in sect. 2, below.

[6] See A. H. Hansen, *Economic Stabilization in an Unbalanced World,* Harcourt,

cisely, that it decreased the amount they desired to spend on goods and services at any given levels of interest rates, prices, and income, which has, as its counterpart, that it increased the amount they wanted to add to their money balances. Such effects on desired flows were presumably accompanied by a corresponding effect on desired balance sheets, namely, a shift away from stocks and toward bonds, away from securities of all kinds and toward money holdings.

The sharp decline in velocity—by 13 per cent from 1929 to 1930—and the turnaround in interest rates are consistent with this interpretation though by no means conclusive, since both declines represent fairly typical cyclical reactions. We have seen that velocity usually declines during contraction, and the more so, the sharper the contraction. For example, velocity declined by 10 per cent from 1907 to 1908, by 13 per cent from 1913 to 1914, and by 15 per cent from 1920 to 1921—though it should be noted that the banking panic in 1907, the outbreak of war in 1914, and the commodity price collapse in 1920 may well have had the same kind of effect on the demand for money as the stock market crash in 1929 had. In contraction years that were both milder and unmarked by such events—1910–11, 1923–24, and 1926–27—velocity declined by only 4 to 5 per cent. It seems likely that at least part of the much sharper declines in velocity in the other years was a consequence of the special events listed, rather than simply a reflection of unusually sharp declines in money income produced by other forces. If so, the stock market crash made the decline in income sharper than it otherwise would have been. Certainly, the coincidence in timing of the stock market crash and of the change in the severity of the contraction supports that view.

Whatever its magnitude, the downward pressure on income produced by the effects of the stock market crash on expectations and willingness to spend—effects that can all be summarized in an independent decline in velocity—was strongly reinforced by the behavior of the stock of money. Compared to the collapse in the next two years, the decline in the stock of money up to October 1930 seems mild. Viewed in a longer perspective, it was sizable indeed. From the cyclical peak in August 1929—to avoid the sharp wiggle in the stock of money produced by the immediate effects of the stock market crash—the money stock declined 2.6 per cent to October 1930, a larger decline than during the whole of all but four preceding reference cycle contractions—1873–79, 1893–94,[7] 1907–08, and

Brace, 1932, pp. 111–112; J. A. Schumpeter, *Business Cycles,* McGraw-Hill, 1939, Vol. II, pp. 679–680; R. A. Gordon, *Business Fluctuations,* Harper, 1952, pp. 377–379, 388; J. K. Galbraith, *The Great Crash, 1929,* Boston, Houghton Mifflin, 1955, pp. 191–192. See also Federal Reserve Board, *Annual Report* for 1929, p. 12.

[7] Since only June estimates of the money stock are available for those years, the

1920–21—and all the exceptions are contractions that were extraordinarily severe by other indications as well. The decline was also larger than in all succeeding reference cycle contractions, though only slightly larger than in 1937–38, the only later contraction comparable in severity to the earlier ones listed.

The decline in the stock of money is especially notable because it took place in a monetary and banking environment that was in other respects free of marked difficulties. There was no sign of any distrust of banks on the part of depositors, or of fear of such distrust on the part of banks. As Chart 27 shows, currency held by the public declined by a larger percentage than deposits—8 per cent compared with 2 per cent—though the reverse relation had been an invariable accompaniment of earlier banking crises. Similarly, the banks made no special effort to strengthen their own liquidity position. Excess reserves—for which no estimates are available before 1929—remained negligible. As we shall see in more detail in the next section, the decline in the stock of money up to October 1930 reflected entirely a decline in Federal Reserve credit outstanding which more than offset a rise in the gold stock and a slight shift by the public from currency to deposits.

ONSET OF FIRST BANKING CRISIS, OCTOBER 1930

In October 1930, the monetary character of the contraction changed dramatically—a change reflected in Chart 30 by the extraordinary rise in the deposits of suspended banks. Before October 1930, deposits of suspended banks had been somewhat higher than during most of 1929 but not out of line with experience during the preceding decade. In November 1930, they were more than double the highest value recorded since the start of monthly data in 1921. A crop of bank failures, particularly in Missouri, Indiana, Illinois, Iowa, Arkansas, and North Carolina, led to widespread attempts to convert demand and time deposits into currency, and also, to a much lesser extent, into postal savings deposits.[8] A contagion of fear spread among depositors, starting from the agricultural areas, which had experienced the heaviest impact of bank failures in the twenties. But such contagion knows no geographical limits. The failure of 256 banks with $180 million of deposits in November 1930 was followed by the failure of 352 with over $370 million of deposits in De-

---

decline was measured from June 1892 to June 1894 rather than from Jan. 1893 to June 1894, the monthly reference dates.

In view of the 5.4 per cent decline in the money stock from Jan. 1867 to Jan. 1868—the earliest dates for which we have estimates—another possible exception is the reference contraction from Apr. 1865 to Dec. 1867.

[8] The growth of postal savings deposits from 1929 to 1933 is one measure of the spread of distrust of banks. In Nov. 1914 postal savings deposits were $57 million. By Aug. 1929 they had grown by only $100 million. By Oct. 1930 they were $190 million; from then to Mar. 1933 they increased to $1.1 billion.

CHART 30

Deposits of Suspended Commercial Banks, Monthly,
1929–February 1933

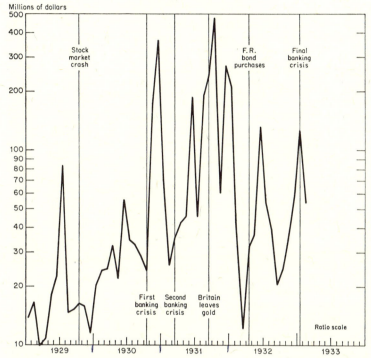

SOURCE: Data from *Federal Reserve Bulletin,* Sept. 1937, p. 909, were adjusted for seasonal variations by the monthly mean method, applied 1921–33.

cember (all figures seasonally unadjusted), the most dramatic being the failure on December 11 of the Bank of United States with over $200 million of deposits.[9] That failure was of especial importance. The Bank of

[9] *Annual Report of Superintendent of Banks,* State of New York, Part I, Dec. 31, 1930, p. 46.

For two and a half months before its closing, Joseph A. Broderick, New York State Superintendent of Banks, had sponsored various merger plans—some virtually to the point of consummation—which would have saved the bank. Governor Harrison devised the final reorganization plan, the success of which seemed so sure that, two days before the bank closed, the Federal Reserve Bank had issued a statement naming proposed directors for the merger. The plan would have become operative had not the Clearing House banks at the last moment withdrawn from the arrangement whereby they would have subscribed $30 million in new capital funds to the reorganized institution. Under Harrison's plan, the Bank of United States would have merged with Manufacturers Trust, Public National, and International Trust—a group of banks that had a majority of stockholders and

United States was the largest commercial bank, as measured by volume of deposits, ever to have failed up to that time in U.S. history. Moreover, though an ordinary commercial bank, its name had led many at

---

directors of the same ethnic origin and social and financial background as most of the stockholders and directors of the Bank of United States—with J. Herbert Case, chairman of the board and Federal Reserve agent of the New York Bank, as head. The decision of the Clearing House banks not to save the Bank of United States was reached at a meeting held at the New York Bank and was not changed despite personal appeals by Broderick and New York State Lieutenant Governor Herbert H. Lehman. Broderick, after waiting in an anteroom for hours despite repeated requests to be allowed to join the bankers in their conference room, was finally admitted through the intercession of Thomas W. Lamont, of J. P. Morgan and Company, and Owen D. Young, a director of the New York Federal Reserve Bank. Broderick's account of his statement of the bankers follows in part:

I said it [the Bank of United States] had thousands of borrowers, that it financed small merchants, especially Jewish merchants, and that its closing might and probably would result in widespread bankruptcy among those it served. I warned that its closing would result in the closing of at least 10 other banks in the city and that it might even affect the savings banks. The influence of the closing might even extend outside the city, I told them.

I reminded them that only two or three weeks before they had rescued two of the largest private bankers of the city and had willingly put up the money needed. I recalled that only seven or eight years before that they had come to the aid of one of the biggest trust companies in New York, putting up many times the sum needed to save the Bank of United States but only after some of their heads had been knocked together.

I asked them if their decision to drop the plan was still final. They told me it was. Then I warned them that they were making the most colossal mistake in the banking history of New York.

Broderick's warning failed to impress Jackson Reynolds, president of the First National Bank and of the Clearing House Association, who informed Broderick that the effect of the closing would be only "local."

It was not the actual collapse of the reorganization plan but runs on several of the bank's branches, which had started on Dec. 9 and which he believed would become increasingly serious, that led Broderick to order the closing of the bank to conserve its assets. At a meeting with the directors after leaving the conference with the bankers, Broderick recalled that he said: "I considered the bank solvent as a going concern and . . . I was at a loss to understand the attitude of askance which the Clearing House banks had adopted toward the real estate holdings of the Bank of United States. I told them I thought it was because none of the other banks had ever been interested in this field and therefore knew nothing of it." Until that time, he said he never had proper reason to close the bank.

Broderick did succeed in persuading the conference of bankers to approve immediately the pending applications for membership in the Clearing House of two of the banks in the proposed merger, so that they would have the full resources of the Clearing House when the next day he announced the closing of the Bank of United States. As a result, the two banks, which like the Bank of United States had been affected by runs, did not succumb.

The details of the effort to save the bank were revealed in the second of two trials of Broderick upon his indictment by a New York County grand jury for alleged neglect of duty in failing to close the bank before he did. The first proceedings ended in a mistrial in Feb. 1932. Broderick was acquitted on May 28. See *Commercial and Financial Chronicle,* May 21, 1932, pp. 3744–3745 for the quotations; also June 4, 1932, p. 4087, for Harrison's testimony.

home and abroad to regard it somehow as an official bank, hence its failure constituted more of a blow to confidence than would have been administered by the fall of a bank with a less distinctive name. In addition, it was a member of the Federal Reserve System. The withdrawal of support by the Clearing House banks from the concerted measures sponsored by the Federal Reserve Bank of New York to save the bank—measures of a kind the banking community had often taken in similar circumstances in the past—was a serious blow to the System's prestige (see section 3, below).

The change in the character of the contraction is reflected clearly in Chart 27. Currency held by the public stopped declining and started to rise, so that deposits and currency began to move in opposite directions, as in earlier banking crises. Banks reacted as they always had under such circumstances, each seeking to strengthen its own liquidity position. Despite the withdrawal of deposits, which worked to deplete reserves, there was a small increase in seasonally adjusted reserves, so the ratio of deposits to bank reserves declined sharply from October 1930 to January 1931.

We have already expressed the view (pp. 167–168) that under the pre-Federal Reserve banking system, the final months of 1930 would probably have seen a restriction, of the kind that occurred in 1907, of convertibility of deposits into currency. By cutting the vicious circle set in train by the search for liquidity, restriction would almost certainly have prevented the subsequent waves of bank failures that were destined to come in 1931, 1932, and 1933, just as restriction in 1893 and 1907 had quickly ended bank suspensions arising primarily from lack of liquidity. Indeed, under such circumstances, the Bank of United States itself might have been able to reopen, as the Knickerbocker Trust Company did in 1908. After all, the Bank of United States ultimately paid off 83.5 per cent of its adjusted liabilities at its closing on December 11, 1930, despite its having to liquidate so large a fraction of its assets during the extraordinarily difficult financial conditions that prevailed during the next two years.[10]

As it was, the existence of the Reserve System prevented concerted restriction, both directly and indirectly: directly, by reducing the concern of stronger banks, which had in the past typically taken the lead in such a concerted move, since the System provided them with an escape mechanism in the form of discounting; and indirectly, by supporting the general assumption that such a move was made unnecessary by the establishment of the System. The private moves taken to shore up the

---

[10] *Annual Report of Superintendent of Banks,* State of New York, Part 1, 1931–45, Schedule E in each report. Four-fifths of the total recovered by depositors and other creditors was paid out within two years of the bank's closing.

banking system were therefore extremely limited.[11] The result was that the episode, instead of being the climactic phase of the banking difficulties, was only the first of a series of liquidity crises that was to characterize the rest of the contraction and was not to terminate until the banking holiday of March 1933.

The initial crisis did not last long. Bank failures declined sharply in early 1931, and the banks' scramble for liquidity came to a halt. There was a marked rise in the ratio of deposits to reserves from January 1931 to March 1931, the terminal month of the segment we have been discussing and the month of the onset of the second banking crisis. In January and February, the public slackened its demand for additional currency; demand and time deposits, after declining in January, rose a trifle in February and held nearly constant in March.

Interest rates show clearly the effects of the banking crisis. Until September 1930, the month before the first banking crisis, both long- and short-term interest rates had been declining, and so had the yields on corporate Baa bonds. Synchronous with the first crisis, a widening differential began to emerge between yields on lower-grade corporate bonds and on government bonds. The yields on corporate bonds rose sharply, the yields on government bonds continued to fall. The reason is clear. In their search for liquidity, banks and others were inclined first to dispose of their lower-grade bonds; the very desire for liquidity made government bonds ever more desirable as secondary reserves; hence the yield on lower-grade securities rose, which is to say, their prices fell, while the yields on government bonds fell. The decline in bond prices itself contributed, as we shall see in more detail later, to the subsequent banking crises. It made banks more fearful of holding bonds and so fostered declines in prices. By reducing the market value of the bond portfolios of banks, declines in bond prices in turn reduced the margin of capital as evaluated by bank examiners, and in this way contributed to subsequent bank failures.[12] The end of the first banking crisis was registered

[11] In some communities financial reconstruction was attempted by arrangements for a strong bank to merge with a weakened bank or, if several weakened banks were involved, by establishing a new institution with additional capital to take over the liabilities of the failing banks, the stockholders of which took a loss (F. Cyril James, *The Growth of Chicago Banks,* New York, Harper, 1938, Vol. II, pp. 994–995).

[12] According to a memorandum, dated Dec. 19, 1930, prepared for the executive committee of the Open Market Policy Conference, banks "dumped securities to make their positions more liquid," thus increasing the pressure on the bond market. Weak bond prices in turn produced "a substantial depreciation in the investment portfolios of many banks, in some cases causing an impairment of capital." In addition, the bond market was almost completely closed to new issues (George L. Harrison Papers on the Federal Reserve System, Columbia University Library, Harrison, Open Market, Vol. I, Dec. 19, 1930; for a full description of the Papers, see Chap. 5, footnote 41 and the accompanying text).

in a sharp improvement in the bond market after the turn of the year; the onset of the next crisis, in renewed deterioration.

The onset of the first liquidity crisis left no clear imprint on the broad economic series shown in Chart 28. However, after the turn of the year, there were signs of improvement in those indicators of economic activity—no doubt partly cause and partly effect of the contemporaneous minor improvement in the monetary area. Industrial production rose from January to April. Factory employment, seasonally adjusted, which had fallen uninterruptedly since August 1929, continued to fall but at a much reduced rate: in all but one month from August 1929 to February 1931, the decline was equal to or greater than the total decline in the three months from February to May 1931. Other indicators of physical activity tell a similar story. Personal income rose sharply, by 6 per cent from February to April 1931, but this is a misleading index since the rise was produced largely by government distributions to veterans.[13] All in all, the figures for the first four or five months of 1931, if examined without reference to what actually followed, have many of the earmarks of the bottom of a cycle and the beginning of revival.

Perhaps if those tentative stirrings of revival had been reinforced by a vigorous expansion in the stock of money, they could have been converted into sustained recovery. But that was not to be. The effects of returning confidence on the part of the public and the banks, which made for monetary expansion by raising the ratios of deposits to currency and to reserves, were largely offset by a reduction in Federal Reserve credit outstanding (see section 5, below). Consequently, the total stock of money was less than 1 per cent higher in March than in January 1931, and lower in March than it had been in December 1930. In March, a second banking crisis started a renewed decline in the stock of money and at an accelerated rate. A month or two later, a renewed decline started in economic activity in general, and the hope of revival that season was ended.

ONSET OF SECOND BANKING CRISIS, MARCH 1931

As Chart 30 shows, deposits of suspended banks began to rise in March, reaching a high point in June. From March on, the public resumed converting deposits into currency, and from April on, banks started strengthening their reserve position, liquidating available assets in order to meet both the public's demand for currency and their own desire for liquidity. Excess reserves, which in January 1931 had for the first time since 1929,

[13] U.S. advances to veterans of World War I of up to 50 per cent of the face value of their adjusted service certificates were made possible by legislation of Feb. 27, 1931. These loans totaled $796 million in the first four months after the enactment.

when data become available, reached the $100 million level and had then declined as confidence was restored, again rose, reaching a level of $125–$130 million in June and July.[14] Once bitten, twice shy, both depositors and bankers were bound to react more vigorously to any new eruption of bank failures or banking difficulties than they did in the final months of 1930.

Events abroad still further intensified the financial weakness—a feedback effect, since the events were themselves largely a response to the prior severe economic and monetary decline in the United States which reduced markets for both goods and services and for foreign securities. The failure in May 1931 of the Kreditanstalt, Austria's largest private bank, had repercussions that spread throughout the continent. It was followed by the closing of banks in Germany on July 14 and 15, as well as in other countries, and the freezing of British short-term assets in Germany. A one-year intergovernmental debt moratorium, and a "standstill agreement" among commercial banks not to press for repayment of short-term international credits, both proposed by President Hoover and agreed to in July,[15] gave the countries involved only temporary relief, as did strict control of foreign exchanges by Germany and borrowing by Britain in France and the United States.

These events had mixed effects on the monetary situation in the United States. On the one hand, they stimulated a flight of capital to the United States, which added to the already swollen gold stock. On the other hand, U.S. commercial banks held a large amount of short-term obligations of foreign banks which were now frozen. Furthermore, financial panic is no respecter of national frontiers. The failure of world-famous financial institutions and the widespread closing of banks in a great country could not but render depositors throughout the world uneasy and enhance the desire of bankers everywhere to strengthen their positions.

The downward pressure on the money stock arising from attempts by depositors to convert deposits into currency and by banks to add to their reserves relative to their liabilities was offset to some extent by the gold inflow from abroad. But this was the only offset. Federal Reserve credit outstanding showed only its usual seasonal movements, though minor open market purchases were undertaken, June–August, to ease the market (see section 5, below). In all, from February to mid-August, there was no net change in Federal Reserve credit outstanding, despite an unprecedented liquidation of the commercial banking system.

The result was that the second banking crisis had far more severe effects on the stock of money than the first. In the six months from

[14] *Banking and Monetary Statistics*, p. 371.

[15] Herbert Hoover, *Memoirs, The Great Depression, 1929–1941*, Macmillan, 1952, pp. 61–80.

February to August 1931, commercial bank deposits fell by $2.7 billion or nearly 7 per cent, more than in the whole eighteen-month period from the cyclical peak in August 1929 to February 1931. In the seven months from February to September 1931, commercial bank deposits fell by 9 per cent, one percentage point more than the maximum decline in deposits during the whole of the 1920–21 contraction. Currency in the hands of the public increased, absorbing the increase in gold and the decline in reserves, so that the total stock of money fell by a smaller percentage than deposits did. Even so, it fell by nearly 5½ per cent from February to August 1931, or at a rate of 11 per cent per year.

The effects of the banking crisis on interest rates show up clearly in the renewed and far more drastic rise in yields on lower-grade corporate bonds, as banks sought to realize on their portfolios and in the process forced bond prices ever lower. By that time, too, the economic contraction had seriously impaired the earning power of many concerns and sharply raised the chances of default. Yields on long-term government bonds continued to fall and reached extraordinarily low levels in mid-1931; so the yield differential rose as a result of a movement in both low- and high-grade securities. One reason, already cited, was that the very desire for liquidity served to enhance the value of government securities. Another was that those securities could be used as collateral for loans from Federal Reserve Banks, hence the decline in Federal Reserve discount rates served to make them more attractive as a secondary reserve. Yields on commercial paper also fell, keeping nearly a stable relation to discount rates.

BRITAIN'S DEPARTURE FROM GOLD, SEPTEMBER 1931

The climax of the foreign difficulties came on September 21, when, after runs on sterling precipitated by France and the Netherlands, Britain abandoned the gold standard.[16] Anticipating similar action on the part

[16] Some 25 other countries followed Britain's lead within the following year. The currencies of about a dozen—the sterling area within which British financial and economic influence remained dominant—moved in general conformity with sterling.

Because of the weakness in sterling immediately after the departure from gold, there was no internal relaxation of orthodox financial standards for several months: Britain balanced her budget and repaid foreign credits; Bank rate went up to 6 per cent on the date of suspension and was not reduced until February 1932, when it was changed to 5 per cent. From that point on, defense of sterling was in general no longer considered necessary; instead, control was substituted to prevent a rise in sterling exchange that, it was feared, would eliminate the stimulus a low rate was expected to give to British exports. Imports were restricted by a new protective tariff passed in February. Accompanying the protective tariff policy was a cheap money policy, adopted originally to facilitate refunding wartime issues at lower rates. An expansion in bank credit began in the second quarter of 1932; the trough of the British business contraction was reached in August 1932, according to NBER reference cycle chronology.

of the United States, central banks and private holders in a number of countries—notably France, Belgium, Switzerland, Sweden, and the Netherlands—converted substantial amounts of their dollar assets in the New York money market to gold between September 16 and October 28. Because of the low level of money-market interest rates in the United States, foreign central banks had for some time been selling dollar bankers' acceptances previously purchased for their accounts by the New York Reserve Bank, the proceeds of which were credited to their dollar bank deposits. From the week of September 16, the unloading of the bills onto the Federal Reserve assumed panic proportions. Foreign central banks drew down their deposits to increase earmarkings of gold, much of which was exported during the following six weeks. From September 16 to September 30, the gold stock declined by $275 million, from then to the end of October by an additional $450 million. Those losses about offset the net influx during the preceding two years and brought the gold stock back roughly to its average level during 1929.

The onset of the external drain was preceded and accompanied by an intensification of the internal drain on the banking system. In August, deposits of suspended banks rose to a level that had been exceeded only in the month of December 1930, and in September rose higher yet. In those two months alone, banks with deposits of $414 million, or more than 1 per cent of the by-then shrunken total of commercial bank deposits, closed their doors. The outflow of gold in September added to the pressure on bank reserves. Currency was being withdrawn internally by depositors justifiably fearful for the safety of banks, and gold was being withdrawn externally by foreigners fearful for the maintenance of the gold standard. The combination of an external drain and an internal drain, and particularly their joint occurrence in the autumn when the demand for currency was in any event at its seasonal peak, was precisely the set of circumstances that in pre-Federal Reserve days would have produced restriction of convertibility of deposits into currency. If the pre-Federal Reserve banking system had been in effect, all other events had been as they were, and restriction of payments by banks had not taken place in December 1930, restriction almost certainly would have occurred in September 1931 and very likely would have prevented at least the subsequent bank failures.[17]

[17] Men who had experienced the 1907 panic were not unmindful of lessons to be learned from it. Samuel Reyburn (president of Lord and Taylor, a New York City department store, and a director of the New York Federal Reserve Bank) suggested at a board meeting in Dec. 1931 "that if the banking difficulties extended much further, it would be possible for the banks to suspend cash payments as they did in 1907, but still continue in business." He believed there would be a difficulty, "which had not been present in 1907, that the Federal reserve banks cannot suspend cash payments." In Mar. 1933, this turned out not to be a

The Federal Reserve System reacted vigorously and promptly to the external drain, as it had not to the previous internal drain. On October 9, the Reserve Bank of New York raised its rediscount rate to 2½ per cent and on October 16, to 3½ per cent—the sharpest rise within so brief a period in the whole history of the System, before or since. The move was followed by a cessation of the external drain in the next two weeks. The gold stock reached its trough at the end of October, and thereafter rose until a renewed gold drain began at the end of December. But the move also intensified internal financial difficulties and was accompanied by a spectacular increase in bank failures and in runs on banks. In October alone, 522 commercial banks with $471 million of deposits closed their doors, and in the next three months, 875 additional banks with $564 million of deposits. All told, in the six months from August 1931 through January 1932, 1,860 banks with deposits of $1,449 million suspended operations,[18] and the deposits of those banks that managed to keep afloat fell by a much larger sum. Total deposits fell over the six-month period by nearly five times the deposits in suspended banks or by no less than 17 per cent of the initial level of deposits in operating banks.

The rise in currency offset some of the effect on the money stock of the decline in deposits. But the offset was minor. The money stock fell

---

problem; the Reserve Banks joined the other banks in restricting payments. One Bank officer commented that "there is the further difference between 1907 and the present time, that the difficulty of the banks in 1907 was not one of solvency, but inability to continue to pay out currency, whereas at the present time the banks are able to pay out currency in large amounts, if necessary, but there is the danger that they may become insolvent in so doing" (Harrison, Notes, Vol. II, Dec. 7, 1931).

That answer was hardly to the point, confusing the problem of the individual bank with the problem of the banking system. The threat of insolvency arose from the inability of the banking system as a whole to pay out currency without a reduction in total deposits, given the failure of the Federal Reserve System to create sufficient additional high-powered money. The attempted liquidation of assets to acquire the high-powered money drove down their prices and rendered insolvent banks that would otherwise have been entirely solvent. By cutting short this process, the early restriction of payments prevented the transformation of a temporary liquidity problem into a problem of insolvency.

[18] Rumors about the condition of some of the largest and best-known New York City banks spread alarm in Europe (Harrison, Conversations, Vol. I, Oct. 2, 1931). However, Harrison considered their position in October 1931 "stronger and more liquid than for a long time." The 23 New York Clearing House banks were not included in a memorandum, dated Dec. 8, 1931, listing the shrinkage in capital funds of the member banks in the second Federal Reserve District, which Harrison sent to Governor Meyer (Miscellaneous, Vol. I, Dec. 8, 1931). The shrinkage ranged from 56 per cent for the highest quality group of banks to more than double the capital funds for the lowest quality group. One of the reasons New York City banks were said to be reluctant to borrow from the Reserve Bank was the fear that Europeans would interpret borrowings as an indication of weakness.

by 12 per cent from August 1931 to January 1932, or at the annual rate of 31 per cent—a rate of decline larger by far than for any other comparable span in the 53 years for which we have monthly data,[19] and in the whole 93-year period for which we have a continuous series on the money stock.

Why should the gold drain and the subsequent rise in discount rates have intensified the domestic financial difficulties so greatly? They would not have done so, if they had been accompanied by extensive open market purchases designed to offset the effect of the external gold drain on high-powered money, and of the internal currency drain on bank reserves. Unfortunately, purchases were not made. The Reserve System's holdings of government securities were actually reduced by $15 million in the six-week period from mid-September to the end of October, and then kept unchanged until mid-December. Though the System raised bill buying rates along with discount rates, it did buy some $500 million additional bills in the crucial six-week period. However, that amount was inadequate to offset even the outflow of gold, let alone the internal drain. The result was that the banks found their reserves being drained from two directions—by export of gold and by internal demands for currency. They had only two recourses: to borrow from the Reserve System and to dump their assets on the market. They did both, though neither was a satisfactory solution.

Discounts rose to a level not reached since 1929, despite the rise in discount rates. The situation and its effects are well described in a memorandum prepared for a meeting of the Open Market Policy Conference in February 1932. The conditions it described were still much the same as those that had prevailed in October 1931.

. . . The weight of these discounts is falling most heavily on banks outside the principal centers. In fact, the discounts of these groups of banks are considerably larger than they were in 1929 when the reserve system was exerting the maximum of pressure for deflation. The present amount of member bank borrowing has always proved deflationary, except perhaps during the war, and with the present sensitive psychology, an interruption to deflation seems unlikely as long as the weight of discounts is as heavy as at present.[20]

The aversion to borrowing by banks, which the Reserve System had tried to strengthen during the twenties, was still greater at a time when depositors were fearful for the safety of every bank and were scrtinizing balance sheets with great care to see which banks were likely to be the

[19] Excluding only the five 5-month intervals spanning the holiday, Oct. 1932-Mar. 1933—Feb.-July 1933, when the recorded data show a decline of the same order of magnitude as the annual rate of decline, Aug. 1931-Jan. 1932. As we shall see in Chap. 8, sect. 1, the banking holiday produced a discontinuity in the money figures, and the recorded decline may be a statistical artifact.

[20] Harrison, Open Market, Vol. II, memorandum, dated Feb. 23, 1932.

next to go. This is the context of the "sensitive psychology" to which the quotation refers.

The effect of the attempt to realize on assets is vividly displayed in Chart 29. For the first time, yields on long-term government bonds and on commercial paper rose sharply along with the yields on lower-grade corporate securities. Those rises in yields clearly did not reflect the effect of the depression on corporate earnings; they reflected the liquidity crisis and the unwillingness or inability of banks to borrow even more heavily from the Reserve System. There was some discussion at the time, and even more later, attributing the decline in the price of government bonds to the federal deficit (under $0.5 billion in fiscal 1931; $2.5 billion in fiscal 1932), and to the fear of "irresponsible" legislation, but it is hard to believe that those factors had much effect in comparison with the extremely heavy pressure on banks to liquidate their assets. Certainly, the rise in the commercial-paper rate reflected both in timing and amount primarily the movements in the discount rate.

Again, we may draw on a preliminary memorandum for an Open Market Policy Conference, this time in January 1932.

Within a period of a few months United States Government bonds have declined 10 per cent; high grade corporation bonds have declined 20 per cent; and lower grade bonds have shown even larger price declines. Declines of such proportions inevitably have increased greatly the difficulties of many banks, and it has now become apparent that the efforts of individual institutions to strengthen their position have seriously weakened the banking position in general.[21]

Some measures were attempted or proposed for the relief of banking difficulties, for example, measures sponsored by the New York Reserve Bank to encourage a more liberal evaluation of bank assets, to reduce the pressure on railroad bond prices, and to accelerate the liquidation of deposits in closed banks.[22] These were palliatives that would have

[21] *Ibid.,* memorandum, dated Jan. 8, 1932.

[22] (1) The Bank sponsored an attempt to develop a uniform method of valuing bank assets, involving a more liberal procedure to be followed by examiners in estimating depreciation. The Comptroller ruled that national banks would be required to charge off no depreciation on bonds of the four highest ratings, and only 25 per cent of the depreciation on all other bonds, except defaulted issues on which the full depreciation was to be charged off. The rule, however, was applied only to banks whose capital funds would not be wiped out if the entire depreciation of all the investments, together with any losses on other assets, were to be written off. Hence banks most in need of liberal treatment were not helped (Harrison, Notes, Vol. II, Aug. 6, 13, and Dec. 7, 1931). (2) It tried to obtain a revision of the rules governing the list of investments legal for savings banks, insurance companies, and trust funds in New York State. The prospect of the elimination of railroad bonds from the legal list threatened a further decline in their price, as holders bound by the list sold the bonds. As a result, commercial bank holdings of railroad bonds suffered losses (*ibid.,* Aug. 13, 1931). (3) It promoted the formation of a railroad bond pool, to restore bond values, conditional

had little effect, even if they had been fully carried out. More far-reaching proposals came from outside the Reserve System. At the urging of President Hoover, and with only the reluctant cooperation of the banking community, a private National Credit Corporation was created in October 1931 to extend loans to individual banks, associated together in cooperatives in each Federal Reserve district, against security collateral not ordinarily acceptable and against the joint guarantee of the members of the cooperative. The Corporation's loans were, however, limited. In Hoover's words, "After a few weeks of enterprising courage . . . [it] became ultraconservative, then fearful, and finally died. It had not exerted anything like its full possible strength. Its members—and the business world—threw up their hands and asked for governmental action."[23] These arrangements were explicitly patterned after those in the temporary Aldrich-Vreeland Act, which had worked so well in 1914, the one occasion when they were used. On Hoover's recommendation, the Reconstruction Finance Corporation was established in January 1932, with authority to make loans to banks and other financial institutions, as well as to railroads, many of which were in danger of default on their bonded indebtedness.[24] The epidemic of bank failures ended at about the same time as the establishment of the RFC, though the two developments may have been unrelated. In any event, during the rest of 1932, RFC loans to

---

on prior adjustment of railroad costs and income (*ibid.*, Oct. 5, and Dec. 7, 1931; also, Conversations, Vol. I, Dec. 5, 1931). (4) It sought the assistance of a group of member banks to accelerate the liquidation of deposits in closed banks. The going banks were asked to buy the assets of the closed banks, and to make an immediate advance against the assets, so that an agreed percentage of deposits could be paid out promptly to depositors (Harrison, Office, Vol. II, Sept. 11, 1931).

[23] Hoover, *Memoirs,* p. 97. See the copy of the prepared statement—requesting formation of the Corporation—read to a meeting of nineteen New York bankers held at Secretary Mellon's apartment, Sunday, Oct. 4, 1931; Hoover's letter, dated Oct. 5, 1931, to Harrison; and Harrison's answer of Oct. 7 (all in Miscellaneous, Vol. I). Harrison stressed the need for a railroad bond pool, to raise the prices of those bonds in bank assets, as an indispensable measure to help the banks in addition to the formation of the Corporation. Also see Notes, Vol. II. Oct. 5, 12, 15, 1931, for the tepid reception of the Corporation by most of the Bank's directors.

[24] The Emergency Relief and Construction Act of July 21, 1932, which increased the borrowing power of the RFC from $1.5 billion to $3.3 billion in addition to its subscribed capital of $500 million, authorized it to advance up to $300 million at 3 per cent interest to states and territories for unemployment relief; to make loans for self-liquidating public works (little was actually advanced either for relief or public works up to the end of the year); to finance marketing of agricultural products in foreign markets and in the U.S.; and to create a regional credit corporation with capital subscribed by the RFC in any land-bank district. These measures did not prevent the continued fall in farm income and farm land values, the rise in farm foreclosures, and continued forced sales due to tax delinquency.

banks totaled $0.9 billion, and deposits of banks that suspended fluctuated about the level of mid-1930.

The Glass-Steagall Act, passed on February 27, 1932, which had its origins in the Treasury and the White House, was mainly designed to broaden the collateral the Reserve System could hold against Federal Reserve notes, by permitting government bonds as well as eligible paper to serve as collateral.[25] But it also included provisions designed to help individual banks by widening the circumstances under which they could borrow from the System.[26]

In May 1932, a bill to provide federal insurance of deposits in banks was passed by the House of Representatives. It was referred to a sub-committee of the Senate Banking and Currency Committee, of which Carter Glass was chairman, but was never reported out.[27] He had opposed a similar provision at the time of the passage of the original Federal Reserve Act.[28] Glass believed that the solution was reform of the practices of commercial banks and introduced several bills to that end.[29] None received the support of the administration or of the Reserve System, and none was passed.[30]

In July 1932, the Federal Home Loan Bank Act was passed in another attempt to cope with the problem of frozen assets—specifically of home

[25] The provision was to expire on Mar. 3, 1933, but was extended another year on Feb. 3, 1933, and thereafter periodically until made permanent by the act of June 12, 1945.

[26] The Glass-Steagall Act permitted member banks to borrow from the Reserve Banks (at penalty rates) on ineligible assets under specified conditions. With the consent of at least five members of the Federal Reserve Board, notes of groups of five or more member banks with insufficient eligible assets could be discounted. A unit bank with a capital under $5 million was also authorized, in exceptional circumstances, to borrow on ineligible assets with the consent of at least five members of the Federal Reserve Board. The release of funds by these terms was slight. The Emergency Relief and Construction Act of July 21, 1932, therefore permitted the Reserve Banks to discount for individuals, partnerships, and corporations, with no other sources of funds, notes, drafts, and bills of exchange eligible for discount for member banks. Those powers were used to a very limited extent. Discounts for individuals, partnerships, and corporations reached a maximum of $1.4 million in Mar. 1933. Authorization to make those discounts expired July 31, 1936.

[27] House bill 11362 was referred to the Senate Banking and Currency Committee on May 28, 1932 (*Congressional Record,* 72d Cong., 1st sess., p. 11515).

[28] Glass had been chairman of the House Banking and Currency Committee in 1913. The bill passed that year by the Senate included deposit guaranty; the bill passed by the House did not. In the conference, the House conferees succeeded in eliminating that provision (Paul M. Warburg, *The Federal Reserve System,* New York, Macmillan, 1930, Vol. I, p. 128).

[29] In 71st Cong., 2d sess., June 17, 1930, S. 4723, on national banking associations (*Congressional Record,* p. 10973); in 72d Cong., 1st sess., Jan. 21 and Mar. 17, 1932, S. 3215 and S. 4115, on Federal Reserve Banks (*ibid.,* pp. 2403, 6329), also Apr. 18, 1932, S. 4412, on Federal Reserve Banks and national banking associations.

[30] See also footnote 134, below.

financing institutions (i.e., savings and loan associations, savings banks, insurance companies). The act provided for the organization of federal home loan banks to make advances to those institutions on the security of first mortgages they held.

The broader economic indicators in Chart 28 show little effect of the financial developments that followed Britain's departure from gold. Rather, they show a continuous decline from the onset of the second banking crisis in March 1931 right on through mid-1932. If anything, there is some stepping up of the rate of decline, but any acceleration is less notable than the high rate of decline throughout: an annual rate of 31 per cent for personal income, of 14 per cent for wholesale prices, and of 32 per cent for production.

The severity of the depression stimulated many remedial efforts, governmental and nongovernmental, outside the monetary area. A nationwide drive to aid private relief agencies was organized in the fall of 1931 by a committee of seventy, appointed by Hoover and named the President's Unemployment Relief Organization. The unemployed in many states formed self-help and barter organizations, with their own systems of scrip. Hoover expanded federal expenditures on public works, but was concerned about incurring deficits for such a purpose. A committee of twelve, representing the public, industry, and labor, appointed by him in September 1931, opposed a construction program financed by public funds. In Congress, however, there was growing support for increased government expenditures and for monetary expansion, proposals widely castigated by the business and financial community as "greenbackism" and "inflationary." On its part, the business and financial community, and many outside it, regarded federal deficits as a major source of difficulty. Pressure to balance the budget finally resulted in the enactment of a substantial tax rise in June 1932. The strength of that sentiment, which, in light of present-day views, seems hard to credit, is demonstrated by the fact that in the Presidential campaign of 1932, both candidates ran on platforms of financial orthodoxy, promising to balance the federal budget.

BEGINNING OF LARGE-SCALE OPEN MARKET PURCHASES, APRIL 1932

In April 1932, under heavy Congressional pressure (see section 5, below), the System embarked on large-scale open market purchases which raised its security holdings by roughly $1 billion by early August. Ninety-five per cent of the purchases were made before the end of June, and no net purchases were made after August 10. The System's holdings then remained almost exactly constant until after the turn of the year when they were reduced in the usual seasonal pattern. Initially, the purchases served mostly to offset a renewed gold outflow but, after June, they were reinforced by a mild gold inflow. From the time the purchases ended until the end of the year, a continued and stronger gold inflow served in their stead to keep high-powered money rising.

The provision of additional reserves reinforced the effect of the tapering off of bank failures in January and February 1932, referred to above, which was accompanied by a return of currency from circulation from February to May. In the absence of the bond purchases, it is possible that the renewed flurry of bank failures in mid-1932, consisting partly of a wave of over 40 failures in Chicago in June, before the RFC granted a loan to a leading Chicago bank, would have degenerated into a major crisis. As it was, bank failures again subsided, so that the rise in the public's currency holdings from May to July was again followed by a decline.

The combination of the more favorable banking situation and of the bond-purchase program is clearly reflected in the behavior of the stock of money. As Chart 27 shows, the decline in both bank deposits and the stock of money moderated. Demand deposits reached a trough in July, total deposits and the money stock, in September; the following rise was mild. In absolute terms, the changes in the stock of money were small; by comparison with the prior sharp declines, the shift was major.

The effect of the purchase program is even clearer in Chart 29, which shows interest rates. In the first quarter of 1932 the rates had fallen from the peaks reached in December 1931 or January 1932. In the second quarter, however, the corporate Baa bond yield soared to a peak (11.63 per cent in May)—unmatched in the monthly record since 1919—and the yield on long-term government bonds rose slightly. Commercial paper rates continued to decline in the second quarter, the reduction in the discount rate in New York on February 26 having led the commercial paper rate. After the purchase program began, a sharp fall occurred in all the rates. The reduction in the discount rate in New York on June 24 again led the commercial paper rate and, in August, the commercial paper rate fell below the discount rate and remained there, a relation without parallel since the beginning of the Reserve System.

The reversal in the relation between the commercial paper rate and the discount rate marked a major change in the role of discounting, about which we shall have more to say in Chapter 9. Except for a spurt in connection with the 1933 banking panic, discounting was not again to be of major importance until long after the end of World War II. Banks were henceforth to seek safety through "excess" reserves, and later, through government securities whose prices were pegged, not through recourse to borrowing. That change was, of course, a major factor in keeping rates from going even lower. Throughout 1932, for example, yields on long-term government bonds were notably higher than at any time between May 1930 and September 1931.

The tapering off of the decline in the stock of money and the beginning of the purchase program were shortly followed by an equally notable change in the general economic indicators shown in Chart 28. Wholesale prices started rising in July, production in August. Personal income continued to fall but at a much reduced rate. Factory employment, railroad ton-miles, and numerous other indicators of physical activity tell a similar story. All in all, as in early 1931, the data again have many of the earmarks of a cyclical revival. Indeed, some students date the cyclical trough in 1932. Burns and Mitchell, although dating the trough in March 1933, refer to the period as an example of a "double bottom."[31]

There is, of course, no way of knowing that the economic improvement reflected the monetary improvement. But it is entirely clear that the reverse was not the case. Aside from the precedence in time of the monetary improvement, the program of large-scale open market purchases was a deliberative action undertaken by the Reserve System. And it was the major factor accounting for the monetary improvement.

The timing relations, previous experience, and general considerations all make it highly plausible that the economic improvement reflected the influence of the monetary improvement, rather than the only other alternative—that it occurred shortly thereafter entirely by coincidence. We have observed that, in the past, an increase in the rate of monetary growth—in the present case, from rapid decline to mild decline and then mild rise—has invariably preceded a trough in general business. After three years of economic contraction, there must have been many forces in the economy making for revival, and it is reasonable that they could more readily come to fruition in a favorable monetary setting than in the midst of continued financial uncertainty.

THE BANKING PANIC OF 1933

As it happened, the recovery proved only temporary and was followed by a relapse. Once again, banking difficulties were a notable feature of the relapse. A renewed series of bank failures began in the last quarter of 1932, mostly in the Midwest and Far West, and there was a sharp spurt in January involving a wider area. The deposit-currency ratio fell; the stock of money ceased growing and began to fall precipitously after January 1933. Statewide bank holidays spread, increasing the demand for currency. Substitutes for currency were introduced as in earlier panics, offsetting to some extent the decline in the money stock shown in our

[31] A. F. Burns and W. C. Mitchell, *Measuring Business Cycles,* New York, NBER, 1946, pp. 82–83; idem, *Production during the American Business Cycle of 1927–1933,* New York, NBER, Bulletin 61, Nov. 1936, pp. 2 and 4.

estimates.[32] The monetary difficulties were accompanied by a reversal in the movement of interest rates and by a relapse on the economic front. Physical indexes ceased rising and began to fall once again and so did prices and other indicators of business activity.

This time the availability of RFC loans did not stem the rising tide of bank failures, partly because a provision of an act passed in July 1932 was interpreted as requiring publication of the names of banks to which the RFC had made loans in the preceding month, and such publication began in August. The inclusion of a bank's name on the list was correctly interpreted as a sign of weakness, and hence frequently led to runs on the bank. In consequence, banks were fearful of borrowing from the RFC. The damage was further increased in January 1933 when, pursuant to a House resolution, the RFC made public all loans extended before August 1932.[33] When runs on individual banks in Nevada threatened to involve banks throughout the state, a state banking holiday relieving them of the necessity of meeting their obligations to creditors was declared on October 31, 1932. Iowa followed suit under similar circumstances on January 20, 1933; Louisiana declared a holiday on February 3 to aid the banks of the city of New Orleans; and Michigan, on February 14. Congress freed national banks in February from penalties for restricting or deferring withdrawals according to the terms of holidays in the states where they were located. By March 3, holidays had been declared in about half the states.[34] While the holiday halted withdrawals in a given state, it

[32] It has been estimated that probably as much as $1 billion in scrip was in circulation in the United States up through the bank holiday (H. P. Willis and J. M. Chapman, *The Banking Situation,* New York, Columbia University Press, 1934, p. 15). See also Chap. 8, sect. 1.

[33] Hoover asserts in his memoirs that, before signing the bill in question (the Emergency Relief and Construction Act of July 21, 1932), he was assured that the list of borrowers from the RFC would be treated as confidential and would not be published, and that if it had not been for this assurance, he "would probably have had to veto the bill" (*Memoirs,* pp. 110–111).

The law specified only that the RFC make monthly reports to the President of the United States and the Congress on all loans granted the previous month. It was John N. Garner, then Speaker of the House, who in August instructed the Clerk to make the reports public. The Democrats claimed that publication of RFC loans served as a safeguard against favoritism in the distribution of loans. There was also some resentment against Eugene Meyer, chairman of the RFC until July 1932, and Secretary of the Treasury Mills, a member of the board of directors, for not keeping Democratic directors informed about RFC actions (Jesse Jones, *Fifty Billion Dollars,* Macmillan, 1951, pp. 72, 82–83, 517–520). For the House resolution, see *Congressional Record,* Jan. 6, 1933, p. 1362.

[34] Bank holidays, by legislation or executive order, included the following main types: (1) for a designated time local banks under state jurisdiction were forbidden to pay out funds at depositors' request; (2) individual banks were authorized, either on their own initiative or with the consent of the state banking department, to notify their depositors of their determination to restrict withdrawals to a specified amount or proportion of deposits; (3) a percentage of deposits up to which depositors might draw was specified for all the banks in a state.

increased pressure elsewhere, because the banks that had been given temporary relief withdrew funds from their correspondents in other states in order to strengthen their position. In addition, substitutes for bank money became essential, as in past restrictions of convertibility of deposits, and internal exchanges were disrupted. Currency holdings of the public rose $760 million, or about 16 per cent, in the two months from the end of 1932 to February 1933.

The main burden of the internal drain fell on New York City banks. Between February 1 and March 1, interior banks withdrew $760 million in balances they held with those banks. New York City banks reduced their holdings of government securities by $260 million during February— a measure that tightened the money market—and turned to the Reserve Bank for borrowing funds. The situation produced nervousness among the New York banks with their much intensified aversion to borrowing. At the beginning of March they still held $900 million in interbank balances.

Fear of a renewed foreign drain added to the anxiety of both the commercial banks and the Federal Reserve System. Rumors that the incoming administration would devalue—rumors that were later confirmed by the event—led to a speculative accumulation of foreign currencies by private banks and other holders of dollars and to increased earmarkings of gold. For the first time, also, the internal drain partly took the form of a specific demand for gold coin and gold certificates in place of Federal Reserve notes or other currency. Mounting panic at New York City banks on these accounts was reinforced in the first few days of March by heavy withdrawals from savings banks and demands for currency by interior banks.

The Federal Reserve System reacted to these events very much as it had in September 1931. It raised discount rates in February 1933 in reaction to the external drain, and it did not seek to counter either the external or internal drain by any extensive open market purchases. Though it increased its government security holdings in February 1933, after permitting them to decline by nearly $100 million in January, they were only $30 million higher at the time of the banking holiday than they were at the end of December 1932. Again it raised the buying rates on acceptances along with the discount rate, and again bills bought increased but by far less than the concurrent drain on bank reserves. Again, as in September and October 1931, banks were driven to discount at the higher rates and to dump securities on the market, so that interest rates on all categories of securities rose sharply (see Chart 29).

This time the situation was even more serious than in September 1931 because of all that had gone before. In addition, the panic was far more widespread. In the first few days of March, heavy drains of gold, both internal and external, reduced the New York Bank's reserve percentage below its legal limit. On March 3, Governor Harrison informed Governor Meyer of the Federal Reserve Board that "he would not take the responsibility of running this bank with deficient reserves in the absence of legal sanction provided by the Federal Reserve Act." With some reluctance, the Board suspended reserve requirements for thirty days.[35]

The System itself shared in the panic that prevailed in New York. Harrison was eager for a bank holiday, regarding suspension of reserve requirements as an inadequate solution and, on the morning of March 3, recommended a nationwide holiday to Secretary of the Treasury Mills and Governor Meyer. Despite much discussion between New York and Washington, by evening the declaration of a national holiday was ruled out. Harrison then joined the New York Clearing House banks and the State Superintendent of Banks in requesting New York's Governor Lehman to declare a state banking holiday.[36] Lehman did so, effective March 4. Similar action was taken by the governors of Illinois, Massachusetts, New Jersey, and Pennsylvania. On March 4, the Federal Reserve Banks remained closed as did all the leading exchanges. The central banking system, set up primarily to render impossible the restriction of payments by commercial banks, itself joined the commercial banks in a

[35] Harrison, Notes, Vol. III, Mar. 3, 1933.

[36] Harrison regarded suspension of reserve requirements as the least desirable alternative, because the Reserve Bank would still be obliged to pay out gold and currency to hoarders. Another alternative was suspension of specie payments, which he also considered unattractive, because "hysteria and panic might result and there probably would be a run on the banks of the country." He concluded that the best course was to declare a nationwide holiday "which would permit the country to calm down and which would allow time for the passage of legislation to remedy the situation."

In response to Harrison's recommendation, Secretary Mills and Governor Meyer suggested instead a banking holiday in the State of New York. Harrison refused to make such a request of Governor Lehman on the initiative of the New York Bank, because he believed a state holiday would only result in greater confusion, since the New York Bank would still have to pay out gold to foreigners, and the rest of the country's banking system could not function if New York declared a holiday. The directors of the New York Bank adopted a resolution requesting the Federal Reserve Board to urge the President of the United States to proclaim a nationwide holiday on Saturday, Mar. 4, and Monday, Mar. 6. Harrison talked to President Hoover by telephone, but the President would not commit himself. Later that evening, reports were received from Washington that both the President and President-elect had gone to bed and that there was no chance that a national holiday would be declared.

Harrison left the Bank immediately to join a conference at Governor Lehman's home in New York, at which the decision for a state holiday was finally reached. Lehman had advised Harrison earlier in the day that he would declare the holiday if it seemed desirable, but he had been annoyed with the Clearing House banks because they had induced him to make a statement that he would not. Later that day the Clearing House banks had agreed to cooperate if Lehman declared a holiday but would not request him to. They feared it would hurt their prestige if they were represented as seeking a holiday; in that case, "they would rather stay open and take their beating" (ibid.).

more widespread, complete, and economically disturbing restriction of payments than had ever been experienced in the history of the country. One can certainly sympathize with Hoover's comment about that episode: "I concluded [the Reserve Board] was indeed a weak reed for a nation to lean on in time of trouble."[37]

A nationwide banking holiday, which was finally proclaimed after midnight on March 6 by President Roosevelt, closed all banks until March 9 and suspended gold redemption and gold shipments abroad. On March 9, Congress at a special session enacted an Emergency Banking Act confirming the powers assumed by the President in declaring the holiday, provided for a way of dealing with unlicensed banks and authorized emergency issues of Federal Reserve Bank notes to fill currency needs. The President thereupon extended the holiday; it was not terminated until March 13, 14, and 15, depending on the location of the banks, which were authorized to open only if licensed to do so by federal or state banking authorities (for a fuller discussion, see Chapter 8, section 1).

As noted in Chapter 4, section 3, the banking holiday, while of the same species as earlier restrictions of payments in 1814, 1818, 1837, 1839, 1857, 1873, 1893, and 1907, was of a far more virulent genus. To the best of our knowledge, in these earlier restrictions, no substantial number of banks closed down entirely even for a day, let alone for a minimum of six business days.[38] In the earlier restrictions, banks had continued to make loans, transfer deposits by check, and conduct all their usual business except the unlimited conversion of deposits into currency on demand. Indeed, the restriction enabled them to continue such activities and, in some instances, to expand their loans by relieving them from the immediate pressure to acquire currency to meet the demands of their depositors—a pressure that was doomed to be self-defeating for the banking system as a whole except through drastic reduction in the stock of money. True, to prepare themselves for resumption, banks generally tended to reduce the ratio of their deposits to reserves, following restric-

[37] *Memoirs,* p. 212.

[38] Clark Warburton notes: "By the middle 1830's most of the states had adopted or were in the process of developing general banking codes, with the insertion of provisions for severe penalties for failure to pay notes in specie, or had placed such provisions in bank charters when renewing them or granting new ones. Under such provisions, suspension of specie payments meant forfeiture of charters, or at least curtailment of business until specie payments were resumed. In some cases, the latter was permitted by special enactments of state legislatures. Under these conditions, suspension of specie payments provided relief from an immediate banking panic, but led to a process of contraction of the bank-supplied circulating medium" ("Variations in Economic Growth and Banking Developments in the United States from 1835 to 1885," *Journal of Economic History,* Sept. 1958, p. 292). We know of no instance where any legislature or bank supervisory authority declared bank charters to be forfeited as a result of a general restriction of convertibility. Instead, legislation was enacted postponing or relieving bangs of the penalties the law imposed for suspension of specie payments.

tion. But the fall in the deposit-reserve ratio and the resulting downward pressure on the money stock were moderate and gradual and could be largely or wholly offset by expansion in high-powered money through specie inflows.[39] As a result, contraction of the stock of money, when it occurred at all, was relatively mild and usually lasted perhaps a year, not several years as in 1929–33. Restriction was, as we remarked earlier, a therapeutic measure to prevent a cumulation of bank failures arising solely out of liquidity needs that the system as a whole could not possibly satisfy. And restriction succeeded in this respect. In none of the earlier episodes, with the possible exception of the restriction that began in 1839 and continued until 1842,[40] was there any extensive series of bank failures after restriction occurred. Banks failed because they were "unsound," not because they were for the moment illiquid.

Restriction of payments was not, of course, a satisfactory solution to the problem of panics. If the preceding description makes it sound so, it is only by comparison with the vastly less satisfactory resolution of 1930–33. Indeed, the pre-World War I restrictions were regarded as anything but a satisfactory solution by those who experienced them, which is why they produced such strong pressure for monetary and banking reform. Those earlier restrictions were accompanied by a premium on currency, which in effect created two separate media of payments; and by charges imposed by banks in one locality on the remission of funds to other banks at a distance, since local substitutes for money would not

[39] See Bray Hammond, *Banks and Politics in America,* Princeton University Press, 1957, p. 713. Referring to the restriction in 1857 which had occurred in the United States but not in Canada, he states: "As usual, the immediate effect of stopping specie payments in the States was ease. The banks, relieved of having to pay their own debts, ceased their harsh pressure on their borrowers. The general understanding that specie payments must sooner or later be resumed impelled a continuance of liquidation but of milder sort."

[40] It is significant that the extensive bank failures of 1839–42 were associated with a restriction of convertibility that was limited mainly to banks in the West and the South. The banks of New York and New England maintained payments.

We are doubtful that the 1837 restriction is an exception, although Willard L. Thorp's *Business Annals* (New York, NBER, 1926, p. 122) refers to "over six hundred bank failures" in that year—which may, of course, have occurred before restriction came in May. The reliability of this figure is questionable. The only data available on number of banks for the period 1834–63 are those contained in the reports on the condition of the banks, made annually to Congress in compliance with a resolution of 1832 (the figures are reprinted in *Annual Report* of the Comptroller of the Currency, 1876, Appendix, p. 94). The number of banks, according to this source, rose from 713 in 1836 to 788 in 1837, 829 in 1838, and 840 in 1839. This series shows a continued rise, whereas it almost surely would show a decline if the number of failures had been the more than 600 noted by Thorp. The number of banks is doubtless an underestimate and may entirely exclude unincorporated private banks, whereas failures may have been concentrated among the latter. Even so, it seems unlikely that new banks would have been more numerous than failures in 1837 even among the categories covered, if so many banks of all kinds had in fact failed.

serve as means of payment elsewhere in the country and banks were reluctant to part with reserve funds that were generally acceptable. To O. M. W. Sprague, "the dislocation of the domestic exchanges" as a result of restriction was a serious disturbance to the trade of the country.[41]

The term suspension of payments, widely applied to those earlier episodes, is a misnomer. Only one class of payments was suspended, the conversion of deposits into currency, and this class was suspended in order to permit the maintenance of other classes of payments. The term suspension of payments is apt solely for the 1933 episode, which did indeed involve the suspension of all payments and all usual activities by the banking system. Deposits of every kind in banks became unavailable to depositors. Suspension occurred after, rather than before, liquidity pressures had produced a wave of bank failures without precedent. And far from preventing further bank failures, it brought additional bank failures in its train. More than 5,000 banks still in operation when the holiday was declared did not reopen their doors when it ended, and of these, over 2,000 never did thereafter (see Chapter 8, section 1). The "cure" came close to being worse than the disease.

One would be hard put to it indeed to find a more dramatic example of how far the result of legislation can deviate from intention than this contrast between the earlier restrictions of payments and the banking holiday under the Federal Reserve System, set up largely to prevent their repetition.

The facts of the banking panic are straightforward. The immediate reasons for its occurrence are not. Why was tentative recovery followed by relapse? Why after some months of quiet was there renewed pressure on the banking system? The answer is by no means clear.

One important factor was the drastically weakened capital position of the commercial banks, which made them extremely vulnerable to even minor drains. The recorded capital figures were widely recognized as overstating the available capital, because assets were being carried on the books at a value higher than their market value.[42] Federal Reserve open market purchases would have improved the capital position by raising market values, but those purchases ended in August 1932. Alternatively, Reconstruction Finance Corporation funds could have improved the capital position if they had been made available in the form of capital.[43]

[41] *History of Crises Under the National Banking System*, National Monetary Commission, 1910, pp. 75, 206, 291.

[42] See footnote 22 above for the change at the end of 1931 in the Comptroller of the Currency's valuation of bonds in national bank portfolios. State banking authorities followed the Comptroller's procedure.

[43] RFC loans helped in a measure, but since the RFC took the best of a distressed bank's assets as security for a loan, often little was left to meet any further

They were not, however, until the Emergency Banking Act of March 9, 1933, authorized the RFC to invest in the preferred stock or capital notes of commercial banks.

The election campaign may well have been another factor. It was the occasion for a summing up by the Republicans of all the perils to which the financial system had been exposed and which they claimed to have successfully surmounted, while the Democrats predicted worse perils to come if the Republicans were continued in office. Fears concerning the safety of the banking system were heightened not only by the campaign talk, but also by the January 1933 disclosure, as noted above, of names of banks to which the RFC had made loans before August 1932, and by consideration in the Senate that same month of the Glass bill which proposed reform of questionable practices of the banks.

Uncertainty about the economic and, particularly, the monetary policies to be followed by the new administration also contributed to the relapse.[44] In the course of the election campaign Roosevelt had made ambivalent statements which were interpreted—certainly by Senator Glass, among others—as committing himself to the retention of the gold standard at

---

demands by depositors. Many of the banks helped by the RFC failed by March 1933 for lack of sufficient capital. Owen D. Young remarked to the directors of the New York Federal Reserve Bank, "Under present methods a loan from the Reconstruction Finance Corporation is largely used to pay off certain depositors before the bank ultimately closes, leaving the other depositors out on a limb because the Reconstruction Finance Corporation has gutted the bank of collateral in securing its loan. If this is all that is to be accomplished it might have been better to make no loans" (Harrison, Notes, Vol. II, July 7, 1932).

[44] The election was decided in Nov. 1932 but the new President was not inaugurated until Mar. 1933, and this interregnum coincided almost precisely with the initial halt in the tentative recovery and then the sharp downward slide. In his memoirs, Hoover argues that the final banking panic could have been prevented had Roosevelt disavowed any intention to devalue the dollar or unbalance the budget and had Roosevelt cooperated with him, as he repeatedly requested him to do, in joint measures to stem the rising tide of banking difficulties (*Memoirs*, pp. 206–216; J. M. Burns, *Roosevelt: The Lion and the Fox*, New York, Harcourt, Brace, 1956, p. 147).

Roosevelt's view was that people were withdrawing money from the banks not because of lack of confidence in him, but because of lack of confidence in banks; what was needed was reorganization and reform of the banking system, not optimistic statements by him (A. M. Schlesinger, Jr., *The Age of Roosevelt*, Vol. 1, *The Crisis of the Old Order, 1919–1933*, Boston, Houghton Mifflin, 1957, pp. 476–477).

There were measures Hoover might have taken on his own responsibility, but as his administration approached the end he was understandably unwilling to initiate policy without the approval of the incoming administration. A few days before the inauguration, the Treasury and the Federal Reserve Board pressed him to declare a nationwide bank holiday, but he proposed instead an executive order controlling the foreign exchanges and gold withdrawals if Roosevelt would approve. Roosevelt again refused to take joint action with him.

the then existing gold parity.[45] After the election, rumors spread that the new administration planned to devalue, that Roosevelt had been persuaded by George Warren to follow a policy of altering the gold content of the dollar as a means of "reflating" prices. The rumors became particularly widespread in early 1933 and gained credence when Roosevelt refused to deny them. The effect of the rumors and the failure to deny them was that, for the first time in the course of the contraction, the internal drain in part took the form of a demand for gold coin and certificates thereby reinforcing the external drain arising from speculative accumulation of foreign exchange.

The rumors about gold were only one part of the general uncertainty during the interregnum about future financial and economic policy. Under ordinary circumstances, it would have been doubtful that such rumors and such uncertainty could be a major factor accounting for so dramatic and widespread a financial panic. But these were not ordinary circumstances. The uncertainty came after more than three years of severe economic contraction and after more than two years of banking difficulties in which one wave of bank failures had followed another and had left the banking system in a peculiarly vulnerable position. The Federal Reserve itself participated in the general atmosphere of panic. Once the panic started, it fed on itself.

2. *Factors Accounting for Changes in the Stock of Money*

The factors accounting for changes in the stock of money during the four years from 1929 to 1933 are strikingly different from those in the other periods we have examined. Generally, the pattern for high-powered money has impressed itself most strongly on the total stock of money, the behavior of the two deposit ratios serving mainly to alter the tilt of the money stock relative to the tilt of high-powered money. That relation holds in Chart 31 only for the period up to October 1930, the onset of the first banking crisis. Thereafter, the two deposit ratios take command. High-powered money moves in a direction opposite to that of the total stock of money, and not even most of its short-term movements leave an impress on the stock of money.

From August 1929 to March 1933 as a whole, the change in high-powered money alone would have produced a rise of 17½ per cent in the stock of money. The change in the deposit-currency ratio alone would

[45] Frank B. Freidel, *Franklin Delano Roosevelt*, Vol. 3, *The Triumph*, Boston, Little, Brown, 1956, p. 351; Rixey Smith and Norman Beasley, *Carter Glass*, New York, Longmans, Green, 1939, pp. 321–323. When Roosevelt was authorized to reduce the gold content of the dollar under authority of the Thomas amendment to the Agricultural Adjustment Act of May 12, 1933, Glass, who had made an important speech on behalf of Roosevelt during the election campaign, made a vigorous attack on him in the Senate (Smith and Beasley, pp. 349–356).

CHART 31

The Stock of Money and Its Proximate Determinants, Monthly,
1929–March 1933

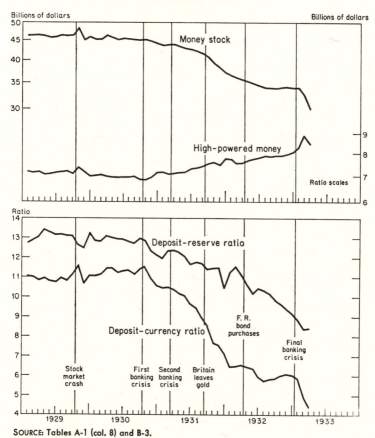

SOURCE: Tables A-1 (col. 8) and B-3.

have produced a decline of 37 per cent; the change in the deposit-reserve
ratio, a decline of 20 per cent; interaction between the two ratios, a rise
of 10 per cent; these three converted the 17½ per cent rise that high-
powered money would have produced into a 35 per cent decline in the
stock of money.[46] For a more detailed examination of these changes, we

[46] The trough of the money stock was reached in April 1933. Although the
percentage decline from Aug. 1929 to Apr. 1933 is only slightly larger than from
Aug. 1929 to Mar. 1933 (35.7 rather than 35.2 per cent), the percentage changes
in the money stock each determinant would have produced if it alone had changed
over the longer period show larger differences: 13, −35, −19, and 9 per cent, in

consider separately each of the periods distinguished in the preceding section and marked off on our charts.

THE STOCK MARKET CRASH, OCTOBER 1929

Before the stock market crash, all three determinants of the money stock, and hence also the money stock itself, had been roughly constant. The constancy in high-powered money reflected a rough constancy in each of the categories into which we have divided the corresponding assets of the monetary authorities: the gold stock, Federal Reserve private claims, and other physical assets and fiat of the monetary authorities (see Chart 32B). However, the constancy of Federal Reserve private claims conceals a not uninteresting detail, brought out by Chart 33, which shows the components of Federal Reserve credit outstanding. The total was roughly constant because a decline in bills discounted was offset by a rise in bills bought. The reason for the divergent movements was the simultaneous rise in August 1929 of the New York Reserve Bank's discount rate from 5 to 6 per cent and the decline of its buying rate on bills (bankers' acceptances) from $5\frac{1}{4}$ to $5\frac{1}{8}$ per cent. We analyzed the reason for these apparently inconsistent movements in the preceding chapter (section 4). Their effect was to make it profitable for banks to get funds from the Reserve System by creating acceptances and selling them to the Reserve Banks rather than by increasing their own indebtedness.

When the crash came, there were widespread attempts by holders of securities to liquidate them and by banks and other lenders outside New York to reduce their loans. As in all such cases, the position of the collection of participants is different from that of any one participant. Long-term securities cannot, on net, be liquidated in a short interval but only

---

the order shown in the text. The reason is that the return flow of currency after the banking holiday reduced high-powered money substantially and also raised the deposit-currency ratio from Mar. to Apr. 1933.

The numerical values of the contributions of the determinants during the contraction, dated as ending in Mar. and in Apr. 1933, follow.

Change in Money Stock That Would Have Been Produced by
Indicated Determinant if It Alone Had Changed

	Rate of Change Per Year (per cent)		Fraction of Total Change	
Proximate Determinant	Aug. 1929– Mar. 1933	Aug. 1929– Apr. 1933	Aug. 1929– Mar. 1933	Aug. 1929– Apr. 1933
High-powered money	4.6	3.2	−0.37	−0.28
Deposit-reserve ratio	−6.2	−5.9	0.52	0.49
Deposit-currency ratio	−13.0	−11.8	1.07	0.98
Interaction	2.6	2.3	−0.22	−0.19
All	−12.1	−12.0	1.00	1.00

Detail may not add to total because of rounding.

transferred from one holder to another. The widespread attempts to liquidate simply reduced prices to a level at which intended purchases matched intended sales.

Loans on securities, especially call loans, are a somewhat more complex affair. In large measure, what is involved is also a transfer of debts from one lender to another, rather than a change in total. But, in addition, the total can be altered much more rapidly. Aside from default, one way is by a transfer of other assets, as most directly when a borrower transfers money to a creditor and reduces his own money balance, or more indirectly when a borrower acquires cash by selling the security serving as collateral to someone else who draws down a money balance to acquire it. Another way is by what is in effect mutual cancellation of reciprocal debts. The most obvious but clearly insignificant example involves the cancellation by two borrowers of loans they have made to one another. A less obvious but more important example involves a longer chain, say, a corporation lending on call in the stock market and simultaneously borrowing from a bank. If the bank takes over the call loan in discharge of its loan to the corporation, the total of the two kinds of debt outstanding is reduced. The total can also be altered by creation of debts; for example, if a corporation lending on call in the market is willing to accept a note from a bank or—more realistically—a deposit in that bank in return for the corporation's claim. In that case, the total of the two kinds of debt is increased.

The essential point for our purpose is that the demand for liquidation of security loans involves one of three arrangements: (1) finding someone willing to take over the loans which, as for securities, can be done by a change of price, that is, a rise in interest rates; (2) finding someone willing to acquire assets for money to be used by the borrower to repay his loan, which can be done by lowering the price of the assets; or (3) arranging for more or less roundabout mutual cancellation or creation of debts, which involves changes in the relative prices of the various assets. The pressure on interest rates and on security prices can be eased by any measure that enhances the supply of funds in one of these forms to facilitate the liquidation of loans in one of these ways.

The situation was eased greatly at the time of the stock market crash by the willingness of New York banks to take over the loans. In the first week after the crash, those banks increased their loans to brokers and dealers by $1 billion and the rest of their loans by $300 million.[47] In large measure, this involved a creation of debts. The former lenders, the "others" for the accounts of whom the New York banks had been making loans, accepted deposits in New York banks as repaying their loans, and the New York banks in turn took over the claims on the bor-

[47] For sources, see footnote 5, above.

CHART 32

High-Powered Money, by Assets and Liabilities of the Treasury
and Federal Reserve Banks, Monthly, 1929–March 1933

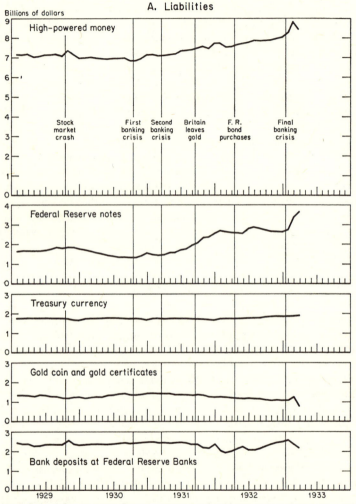

A. Liabilities

NOTE: Federal Reserve notes, Treasury currency, and gold coin and certificates are outside
the Treasury and Federal Reserve Banks.
SOURCE: Same as for Chart 19.

CHART 32 (Concluded)

B. Assets

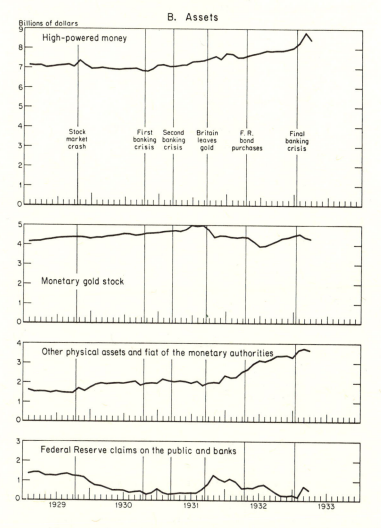

rowers without pressing for their immediate payment. That is the reason the monetary effect of the crash shows up in our money stock series as a sharp increase in demand deposits and the reason the increase was in New York City. Indeed, the increase in our estimates understates the magnitude of the action of the New York banks. Some of the loans taken over

CHART 33
Federal Reserve Credit Outstanding, by Types, Monthly, 1929–March 1933

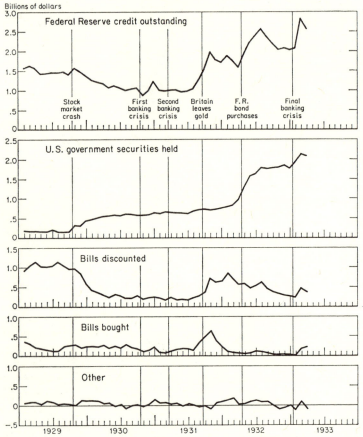

SOURCE: Same as for Chart 22, except that all seasonal adjustments are by Shiskin-Eisenpress method (reference given in source for Chart 21).

were for the accounts of out-of-town banks and were matched by an increase in interbank deposits of $510 million in New York City weekly reporting member banks. But our money stock estimates exclude interbank deposits.

To be able to expand deposits, the New York banks had to be able either to raise the ratio of deposits to reserves or to acquire additional reserves. The first was impossible because New York banks had no excess reserves. Indeed, the ratio of deposits to high-powered reserves was lower in New York than in the rest of the country because of the higher legal reserve requirements imposed on banks in central reserve cities. Therefore the increase in deposits in New York relative to deposits in the rest of the country in October 1929 produced a decline in the average deposit-reserve ratio for the country as a whole. Accordingly, the New York banks had to and did acquire additional reserves, as the bulge in high-powered money shows. They did so in the week of the crash partly by borrowing from the Federal Reserve Bank of New York, which, in Harrison's words, kept its "discount window wide open and let it be known that member banks might borrow freely to establish the reserves required against the large increase in deposits resulting from the taking over of loans called by others;"[48] and partly by virtue of the purchase by the New York Bank of about $160 million of government securities. That purchase was far in excess of the amount the System's Open Market Investment Committee had been authorized to purchase for System account. It was made by the New York Bank on its own initiative for its own account without consulting either the Open Market Investment Committee or the Board. Though subsequently ratified, it was, as we shall see in more detail in section 5, below, the occasion for another battle in the struggle between the Bank and the Board, which had important effects on Federal Reserve policy during the rest of the contraction.

The actions taken by the New York Reserve Bank were timely and effective. Despite the stock market crash, there were no panic increases in money market rates such as those in past market crises, and no indirect effects on confidence in banks which might have arisen if there had been any sizable defaults on security loans. Harrison himself expressed the view that "it is not at all unlikely that had we not bought governments so freely, thus supplementing the reserves built up by large additional discounts, the stock exchange might have had to yield to the tremendous pressure brought to bear upon it to close on some one of those very bad days the last part of October."[49] Harrison may have overstated the case— he was, after all, writing in defense of the actions the New York Bank had taken—but that is by no means certain.

In the month following the crash, there was a reversal. Deposits declined, as more lasting arrangements for the transfer and reduction of stock market loans replaced the temporary shift of many of those loans to New York banks. The changes in deposits produced a decline in the deposit-currency ratio, following the rise in October, and a decline in

[48] Harrison, Miscellaneous, Vol. I, letter, dated Nov. 27, 1929, Harrison to all governors. During the week ending Oct. 30, 1929, discounts increased $200 million at all Reserve Banks, of which $130 million was the increase in New York City weekly reporting member bank borrowings from the New York Reserve Bank.

[49] *Ibid.,* letter, dated Nov. 27, 1929, Harrison to all governors.

the deposit-reserve ratio milder than that in October. High-powered money also declined as a result of a reduction in bills discounted and in the gold stock, generally attributed to the withdrawal by foreigners of funds from the New York money market.[50] The net effect was to leave the stock of money after the crash at a lower level than before. At the end of November 1929, the stock of money was $1.3 billion, or 3 per cent, less than it had been at the end of September. By the end of December, most of the loss had been made up; the stock of money was about $0.5 billion, or 1 per cent, less than in September. These changes were concentrated in demand deposits. From December 1929 to October 1930, the stock of money fluctuated around a roughly constant level though with a mild downward trend. In October 1930, the stock of money was almost the same as it had been in November 1929 and nearly 2 per cent below its level at the end of December 1929.

For the period from August 1929 to October 1930 as a whole, the money stock declined by 2.6 per cent. High-powered money alone declined by 5 per cent. However, the deposit-currency ratio rose by about 7 per cent, enough to offset a minor decline in the deposit-reserve ratio as well as half the decline in high-powered money. In October 1930, the deposit-currency ratio stood at the highest level reached at any time in the 93 years covered by our data, except only for a fractionally higher peak reached in the month of the stock market crash (see Charts 31 and 64, and Table B-3). As we noted earlier, the public was clearly not greatly concerned at the time about the safety of bank deposits. But the high ratio made the System peculiarly vulnerable to the development of any such concern, as the following years were to demonstrate so tragically.

The decline in high-powered money occurred despite an increase of $210 million in the gold stock and of $470 million in the fiat of the monetary authorities. The latter increase reflected mostly a rise in government securities held by the System, i.e., the substitution of noninterest-bearing for interest-bearing government debt. Those expansionary factors were more than offset by a decline in Federal Reserve private claims of $1,020 million—$100 million in bills bought and $920 million in bills discounted and other claims (see Chart 32B). Ultimately then, it was the failure of the Reserve System to replace the decline in discounts by other

---

[50] The return flow of foreign funds gave temporary relief to the foreign exchanges, which had been under pressure during the period of speculation. Foreign currencies had depreciated vis-à-vis the dollar, while foreigners were remitting funds to the security markets here. Before the peak in stock prices in 1929, the prices of those currencies had declined to the United States' gold import point. After the crash, the return flow of funds raised their prices to the gold export point. For example, the pound was as low as $4.845857 in Sept. 1929 and in Dec. was as high as $4.882010 (the figures are noon buying rates for cable transfers to New York, from *Commercial and Financial Chronicle*, Sept. 21, 1929, p. 1969; Dec. 27, 1929, p. 4017).

credit outstanding that was responsible for the decline in the stock of money.

The decline in discounts took place despite sharp reductions in discount rates—at the New York Bank, from 6 per cent to 2½ per cent in June 1930 (Chart 29). The successive declines in discount rates—the first of which came in November 1929, three months after the date set by the National Bureau as the reference cycle peak—though sharp and rapid by earlier standards, took place during a time when there was a sharp decline in the demand for loans and an increase in the demand for assets regarded as safe. Both made for a sharp decline in market interest rates. Though the discount rate fell absolutely, it probably rose relative to the relevant market interest rates, namely, those on short-term securities with essentially zero risk of default. Hence, discounting became less attractive. It is perhaps worth noting that this is not merely a retrospective judgment. The New York Reserve Bank favored more rapid reductions in the rate than those made. Harrison said in May 1931 that "if there had been no Federal Reserve System in October, 1929, money rates would probably have come down more rapidly than they had . . . ." In September 1930, Adolph Miller of the Federal Reserve Board said at a meeting with all the governors, "Money is not really cheap nor easy." In mid-1930, Harold L. Reed, in the second of his two excellent books on the Federal Reserve System said: "In the writer's opinion, however, there was much stronger ground for holding that the rate reductions had been too gradual and long delayed" than that they had been too rapid.[51]

As the near-constancy of the deposit-reserve ratio indicates, there was no tendency of banks to accumulate excess reserves. It has been contended with respect to later years (particularly during the period after 1934, when large excess reserves accumulated) that increases in high-powered money, through expansion of Federal Reserve credit or other means, would simply have been added to bank reserves and would not have been used to increase the money stock. In other words, a rise in high-powered money would have been offset by a decline in the deposit-reserve ratio. We shall argue later that the contention is invalid even for the later period. It is clearly not relevant to the period from August 1929 to October 1930. During that period, additional reserves would almost certainly have been put to use promptly. Hence, the decline in the stock

---

[51] See sect. 5 below for the New York Bank's position. The quotation from Harrison is from Harrison, Notes, Vol. I, May 21, 1931; from Miller, Charles S. Hamlin, Hamlin Papers, Manuscript Division, Library of Congress, Diary, Vol. 18, Sept. 25, 1930, p. 86; from Reed, *Federal Reserve Policy, 1921–1930,* New York, McGraw-Hill, 1930, p. 191. This may not have been Miller's view earlier in the year. In May, Hamlin reported, "Miller said the Federal Reserve Bank of New York was obsessed with the idea that easy money would help the business recession" (Hamlin, Diary, Vol. 17, May 9, 1930, p. 151).

of money is not only arithmetically attributable to the decline in Federal Reserve credit outstanding; it is economically a direct result of that decline.

ONSET OF FIRST BANKING CRISIS, OCTOBER 1930

The onset of the banking crisis is clearly marked in all three proximate determinants but particularly in the deposit ratios (Chart 31). From a peak of 11.5 in October 1930, the ratio of deposits to currency declined sharply—a decline that was to carry the ratio, with only minor interruptions along the way, to a low of 4.4 in March 1933. The deposit-reserve ratio likewise began a decline that was to carry it from a level of 12.9 in October 1930—the all-time high was 13.4 in April 1929—to a level of 8.4 in March 1933. These declines brought the deposit-currency ratio back to its level at the turn of the century and the deposit-reserve ratio to its level in 1912. They thus wiped out the whole of the much heralded spread in the use of deposits and "economy" in reserves achieved under the Reserve System.

The decline in the stock of money as a result of the banking crisis—a decline of slightly more than 3 per cent from October 1930 to January 1931, or more than in the preceding fourteen months—was clearly a result of the declines in the two deposit ratios, since high-powered money rose by 5 per cent. As Charts 32B and 33 show, the rise of $340 million in high-powered money, seasonally adjusted, was produced partly by an inflow of $84 million of gold[52]—the source that had always been the major reliance in pre-Federal Reserve crises—partly by an increase of $117 million in Federal Reserve credit outstanding. The increase in Federal Reserve credit consisted partly of a rise of $41 million in government securities, the balance of a rise in float. A rise in discounts just about offset a decline in bills bought. There was a brief spurt of roughly $200 million in bills discounted in the two weeks after the failure of the Bank of United States, but it does not show up in the seasonally adjusted end-of-month figures plotted in Chart 33.

The rise in Federal Reserve credit certainly helped to offset some of the immediate effects of the banking crisis. But the movement was minor in magnitude. Many an earlier year-end shows rises of comparable magnitude and, even at its peak in December 1930, seasonally adjusted Federal Reserve credit was only 84 per cent of its level in the summer of 1929 when the System was seeking to curb speculation. The one other measure taken by the System in reaction to the banking crisis was a re-

[52] The gold inflows reflected partly the Hawley-Smoot Tariff Act passed in June 1930, which raised the tariff to the highest level up to that time in U.S. history; partly the reduction of U.S. lending abroad, and the continuance at a high level of interest and dividends on investments abroad and of war debt payments; partly the consequence of U.S. deflation on imports and exports. See sect. 4, below.

duction in late December 1930 in the New York Reserve Bank's discount rate to 2 per cent—to reassure the public.[53]

The rise in Federal Reserve Bank credit was temporary. After December 1930, discounts declined, bills bought were allowed to run off without replacement, while government security holdings increased by only a small fraction of the combined decline in discounts and bills bought. High-powered money rose in January 1931, only because a continued gold inflow offset the decline in Federal Reserve credit. It declined in February despite continued gold inflow, and rose slightly in March along with a minor rise in Federal Reserve credit and the gold stock. The decline in Federal Reserve credit from December 1930 to March 1931 was greater than the gold inflow. In effect, the System was not only sterilizing the gold inflow, but exerting a contractionary influence greater than the expansionary influence of the gold inflow.

Despite the reduction in high-powered money in February 1931, the money stock rose a bit because of a rise in both deposit ratios, as the wave of bank failures died down and confidence in banks was somewhat restored. As suggested earlier, if the rises in the deposit ratios had been reinforced by a vigorous expansion in high-powered money, instead of being offset by a reduction, the ground gained might have been consolidated and extended.

ONSET OF SECOND BANKING CRISIS, MARCH 1931

The onset of the second banking crisis is clearly marked in Chart 31 by the renewed decline in the deposit ratios and the beginning of a decline in the money stock at the fastest rate so far in the contraction. In the five months from March to August, to exclude wholly the effects of Britain's departure from gold in September, the stock of money fell by $5\frac{1}{4}$ per cent, or by almost exactly the same percentage as in all the preceding nineteen months of the contraction. This was at the phenomenal annual rate of 13 per cent, yet the rate was soon to rise still higher.

As after the first banking crisis, the decline in the stock of money was entirely a consequence of the fall in the deposit ratios. High-powered money rose, this time by 4 per cent from March to August, and so offset nearly half the contractionary effect of the declining deposit ratios. There were, however, two differences between the second banking crisis and the first one some six months earlier.

[53] Governor Harrison wrote, "he had been urged from many quarters to make a reassuring statement which might aid in quieting the banking situation. Such a statement was practically impossible because to be strong enough to do any good it would run the risk of being contradicted by any small bank failure which might thereafter occur. The rate reduction, apart from other reasons, served as a method of stating to the public that money was freely available" (Harrison, Open Market, Vol. II, Jan. 21, 1931).

(1) This time, the rise in high-powered money was produced almost entirely by the continued gold inflow, whereas earlier there had been at least a temporary increase in Federal Reserve credit, which helped to absorb some of the initial effects of the crisis. Federal Reserve credit remained almost perfectly stable, rising slightly only in July and August 1931. Despite the unprecedented liquidation of the commercial banking system, the books of the "lender of last resort" show a decline in bills discounted from the end of February to the end of April—a period when the usual seasonal movement is upward—and a rise from April to the end of August that made the whole increase from February to August less than th usual seasonal increase; they show irregular increases and decreases in bills bought, with the total at the end of August $75 million higher than at the end of February, but still below its level at the turn of the year; and they show an increase of $130 million in government securities purchased, the whole of the increase beginning late in June. Of this increase, $50 million was a purely technical move rather than a reaction to domestic financial difficulties: it simply offset other reductions in credit outstanding. The remaining $80 million represented a deliberate, if timid, move to contribute ease.[54]

(2) The second crisis lasted longer. In late 1930, there were signs of improvement after two or three months. On this occasion, as Chart 31 shows, the deposit-currency ratio—the most sensitive indicator of the public's attitude toward banks—not only continued to fall, but fell at an increasing rate. There was no sign that the crisis was drawing to an end when Britain's departure from gold intensified it.

Aside from the modest open market purchases in July and August, the only other domestic action of the System relevant to the money stock was a further reduction in the discount rate of the New York Reserve Bank to $1\frac{1}{2}$ per cent in May—before the sharp June increase in bank failures. As we have seen, the reduction did not stimulate borrowing. On a different front, potentially of great consequence for the domestic money stock, the System participated in loans to foreign banks as part of an international effort to avert financial catastrophe abroad.[55]

[54] Federal Reserve Board, *Annual Report* for 1931, pp. 7–8. These figures are all as of Wednesdays. Of the $130 million of government securities purchased, $80 million was for System account and $50 million for the New York Bank's own account (Harrison, Open Market, Vol. II, minutes of June 22 and Aug. 11, 1931, Open Market Policy Conference meetings; Miscellaneous, Vol. I, letter, dated July 9, 1931, Harrison to Seay; Notes, Vol. I, July 16, 1931, and Vol. II, Aug. 4, 1931). The latter purchase was made to offset the effect of the transfer of foreign-held balances from the acceptance market to Federal Reserve Banks.

[55] During the second and third quarters of 1931, the Federal Reserve Bank of New York in association with other Federal Reserve Banks purchased prime commercial bills with guaranteed repayment in gold from the Austrian National Bank, the National Bank of Hungary, the Reichsbank, and the Bank of England. The credit agreements with the Federal Reserve Banks at their separate maximums

BRITAIN'S DEPARTURE FROM GOLD, SEPTEMBER 1931

In the few months after the departure of Britain from the gold standard, the proximate determinants of the money stock plotted in Chart 31 continued the pattern of the preceding five months, but the pattern was even more emphatic. The stock of money fell still faster: in the five months from August 1931 to January 1932, it fell by 12 per cent—compared with 5 per cent in the preceding five months—or at the annual rate of 31 per cent—compared with 13 per cent. High-powered money again rose, this time by about $4\frac{1}{2}$ per cent, and again offset only part, and this time a smaller part, of the effect of the declines in the deposit ratios, particularly the deposit-currency ratio. The banks were so hard pressed to meet the demands of their depositors that, try though they did, they were able to do little to lower the ratio of their deposit liabilities to their reserves. That had to wait for a more propitious time, which is why the most rapid decline in the deposit-reserve ratio came later when the decline in the deposit-currency ratio had tapered off, and the slowest decline came earlier when the deposit-currency ratio was declining fastest. As we shall see in later chapters, much of the adjustment on the part of the banks did not come until after the end of the business contraction and the beginning of recovery. The timing relations between changes in the two deposit ratios during the 1931–32 segment of the contraction repeated the tendencies we have observed in each earlier banking crisis.

The major difference, aside from scale, between the five-month period, August 1931–January 1932, and the preceding five months is the source of the rise in high-powered money, which does not show up in Chart 31 but does in Charts 32B and 33. Up to August 1931, high-powered money had risen chiefly as a result of gold inflows. As noted in section 1 above, the period after Britain's departure from gold saw a sharp outflow, particularly in September and October 1931, large enough to offset

---

aggregated about $156 million and were renewed several times. Reserve Bank holdings of bills payable in foreign currencies increased from $1 million at the end of March to $145 million in August (Federal Reserve Board, *Annual Report* for 1931, pp. 12–13).

See also Harrison, Miscellaneous, Vol. I, letter, dated July 9, 1931, Harrison to McDougal; Open Market, Vol. II, minutes of meeting, Aug. 11, 1931; and Notes, Vol. I, June 1, 15, 22; July 13, 16, 1931; Vol. II, July 28, 30; Aug. 4; Sept. 24, 28, 1931, for discussion of the foreign credits. One of the directors of the New York Reserve Bank, Charles E. Mitchell, was quoted as saying, "In all of these cases, he was concerned about the soundness of the operation to be undertaken by the Federal reserve banks which, in their domestic business, take as few chances as possible," and "the thing which bothered him with regard to these foreign credits was the risk involved when, at home, the Federal reserve banks take no risks" (Harrison, Notes, Vol. I, June 22, 1931).

the gold inflows during the earlier segments of the contraction. High-powered money rose because Federal Reserve credit outstanding rose. Federal Reserve credit rose primarily because of the sharp rise in discounts as banks, having no other recourse open to them, were driven to borrowing from the Reserve System, despite the unprecedentedly sharp rises in discount rates in October 1931. Bills bought increased substantially in September and October, but then were allowed to run off so that, by January 1932, they had fallen below their level at the end of August 1931. All told, from August 1931 to January 1932, the rise of $330 million in high-powered money was accounted for by a rise of $560 million in discounts, $80 million in government securities, $270 million in other assets of the monetary authorities, offset by a decline of $580 million in the gold stock.

During those five months when high-powered money rose by $330 million, currency held by the public increased by $720 million. The extra $390 million had to come from bank reserves. Since banks were unwilling and unable to draw down reserves relative to their deposits,[56] the $390 million, amounting to 12 per cent of their total reserves in August 1931, could be freed for currency use only by a multiple contraction of deposits. The multiple worked out to roughly 14, so deposits fell by $5,727 million or by 15 per cent of their level in August 1931. It was the necessity of reducing deposits by $14 in order to make $1 available for the public to hold as currency that made the loss of confidence in banks so cumulative and so disastrous. Here was the famous multiple expansion process of the banking system in vicious reverse. That phenomenon, too, explains how seemingly minor measures had such major effects. The provision of $400 million of additional high-powered money to meet the currency drain without a decline in bank reserves could have prevented a decline of nearly $6 billion in deposits.

In discussing the 1907 crisis, we showed how the rise in deposit ratios had made the banking system more vulnerable to an attempted conversion of deposits to currency. The situation in 1931 was even more extreme. At no time in 1907 did the public hold more than $6 in deposits for every $1 it held in currency; in March 1931, when the second banking crisis began, it held over $10 in deposits for every $1 of currency, an amount it succeeded in reducing to under $7 by January 1932. In 1907, the banks owned less than $9 in deposits for every $1 of high-powered money they held as reserves; in March 1931, they owed more than $12. The more extensive use of deposits—widely regarded during the twenties as a sign of the great progress and refinement of the American financial structure—and the higher ratio of deposits to reserves—widely regarded as a sign of the effectiveness of the new Reserve System in promoting

[56] At the end of Jan. 1932, their excess reserves totaled $40 million.

"economy" in the use of reserves—made the monetary system much more vulnerable to a widespread loss of confidence in banks. The defenses deliberately constructed against such an eventuality turned out in practice to be far less effective than those that had grown up in the earlier era.

When bank failures tapered off in February and March 1932, the deposit-currency ratio temporarily stopped falling. However, high-powered money declined by $160 million in those two months, despite a dwindling of gold outflows, mainly as a result of changes in Reserve Bank credit: a decline of $280 million in discounts, and a continued decline of $50 million in bills bought, while government security holdings rose by about $180 million. Discounts declined because banks took advantage of the pause in the demands on them to repay some of their borrowings. They followed that course despite a reduction in the New York Bank's discount rate to 3 per cent in February. The banks took advantage of the pause also to strengthen their reserve position somewhat, so the deposit-reserve ratio fell slightly from January to March 1932. The result was that the stock of money continued to decline though at a slower pace. In these two months it fell by another 2 per cent, an annual rate of 13 per cent, which can be described as moderate only by comparison with the preceding 31 per cent annual rate of decline.

BEGINNING OF LARGE-SCALE OPEN MARKET PURCHASES, APRIL 1932

The beginning of the purchase of government securities on a large scale by the Federal Reserve System in April 1932, involving purchase of $350 million during that month (see Chart 33 for seasonally adjusted end-of-the-month figures), had no immediate effect on the behavior of the stock of money. It declined another $4\frac{1}{2}$ per cent for another four months, or at an annual rate of 14 per cent. The decline then slowed up sharply, the money stock falling one-half of 1 per cent in the two months from July to September 1932, or at the annual rate of 3 per cent. From September on, it rose mildly until January 1933, when the money stock was one-half of 1 per cent higher than in September 1932, implying an average rate of growth of about $1\frac{3}{4}$ per cent per year.

The reason the bond purchases had no greater effect to begin with is that they were offset in part by a renewed outflow of gold and the rest was more than offset by continued declines in the deposit ratios. From April to July 1932, when Reserve System holdings of government securities went up by roughly $1 billion, the gold stock fell by about half that amount, most of the outflow going to France. At the same time, a renewed flurry of bank failures in June produced a further appreciable decline in the deposit-currency ratio, and the continued efforts of the banks to strengthen their position produced a further decline in the deposit-reserve ratio.

The gold drain ceased in mid-June and was replaced by an inflow.

Over the rest of the year, the gold stock rose by $600 million, bringing the gold stock in January 1933 above its level a year earlier. Reserve System bond purchases ceased in August 1932. Discounts and bills bought fell from July on, so that total Federal Reserve credit outstanding reached a peak in that month and fell by $500 million from then to January 1933. Nonetheless, high-powered money continued to rise at roughly a constant rate from April 1932 to January 1933 because of the reversal of the gold flow, plus an increase of $140 million in national bank notes. The latter increase was due to an amendment attached to the Home Loan Bank Act of July 1932, which broadened the range of government bonds eligible as security for national bank notes.[57] Once the deposit-currency ratio reached its trough in July 1932, the rise in high-powered money plus the rise in the deposit-currency ratio were enough to offset the continued fall in the deposit-reserve ratio and produce the pattern of change in the money stock already described.

The form taken by the improvement in the banking position, recorded in the deposit-reserve ratio, is worth noting because it presaged a development that was to be important in the next few years. Banks began to accumulate substantial reserves in excess of legal requirements. Since the Reserve System regarded the so-called "excess reserves" as a sign of monetary ease, their accumulation contributed to adoption of the policy of keeping total government securities at the level reached in early August. Excess reserves were interpreted by many as a sign of lack of demand for bank funds, as meaning that monetary authorities could make "credit" available but could not guarantee its use, a position most succinctly conveyed by the saying, "monetary policy is like a string; you can pull on it but you can't push on it." In our view, this interpretation is wrong. The reserves were excess only in a strictly legal sense. The banks had discovered in the course of two traumatic years that neither legal reserves nor the presumed availability of a "lender of last resort" was of much avail in time of trouble, and this lesson was shortly to be driven home yet again. Little wonder that the reserves they found it prudent to hold exceeded substantially the reserves they were legally required to hold.[58] As noted above, their reaction was the same as in

[57] The amendment permitted use for a period of three years of all government bonds bearing interest at 3⅜ per cent or less, including future bond issues during the period. From August 1929 up to July 1932 there was a slight increase—$60 million—in national bank notes in circulation, as national banks exercised somewhat more fully their right to issue on the security of three government bond issues bearing interest at 2 per cent, which had the circulation privilege.

[58] See Chap. 8, sect. 1, for evidence on this view. In Dec. 1932, Governor Meyer said that "if the banks knew that there was going to be a constant amount of excess reserves over a long period, that amount could be relatively small and still be more effective than a much larger but uncertain amount . . . . We have not obtained the full effect of recent large excess reserves because of uncertainty as to our future policy" (Harrison, Notes, Vol. III, Dec. 22, 1932).

earlier crises, only greater in magnitude in response to the greater severity of the crisis.

THE BANKING PANIC OF 1933

The final banking crisis, which terminated in the banking holiday early in March 1933, was in most essential respects a duplicate of the two preceding ones but still more drastic. The money stock fell 12 per cent in the two months from January to March 1933, or at an annual rate of decline of 78 per cent. For reasons we discuss in detail in the next chapter, our estimates overstate the decline in the stock of money, but hardly any reasonable allowance for error could cut the rate of decline to less than the 31 per cent rate of decline from August 1931 to January 1932. As in the earlier crises, high-powered money rose, primarily as a result of a rise in discounts and a lesser rise in bills bought. Chart 33 shows an appreciable rise in government securities. This rise is produced by the seasonal adjustment. There is no rise in the original figures. The early months of the years before 1933 were generally characterized by a decline in the Reserve portfolio of government securities in response to the return flow of currency from circulation usual at that season. In 1933, there was, of course, a drain of currency rather than a return flow: government securities were nevertheless reduced in January by $90 million, but then raised in February by $70 million, to a level at which they also stood at the end of March. Seasonal adjustment of the figures converted the decline in January and the modest rise in February to appreciable increases, and raised the original March figure only slightly less.

The banking holiday in March renders all the money figures noncomparable with earlier ones, so we consider the change from January to February alone, as an approximation of the decline up to the bank holiday. In that one month the money stock fell 4½ per cent, or at an annual rate of 56 per cent. Currency held by the public rose by over $600 million, high-powered money by $535 million—almost the same. But even the remaining $65 million which had to be supplied from bank reserves, plus the scramble by banks for reserves, produced a decline in deposits of over $2 billion in that one month, or nearly 7½ per cent of the already shrunken total. This time the multiplier was not 14 but 29.

The major monetary difference between the final banking crisis and the earlier ones was that for the first time the internal drain in part clearly took the form of a drain of gold coin and certificates. As Chart 32A shows, the volume of gold coin and certificates had risen mildly in 1930 but then had been constant or declining until the onset of the final crisis. In January 1933, the amount of gold coin and gold certificates outside the Treasury and Federal Reserve Banks was $420 million less than at its peak in December 1930, $340 million less than at its previous

January peak in 1931. The decline was apparently in some measure the result of a deliberate policy on the part of the Federal Reserve System of adding to its gold reserves by paying out Federal Reserve notes instead of gold certificates where feasible, a reversal of the policy adopted during the twenties to keep down the apparent reserve ratio (see Chapter 6, section 4).[59] Though the total of gold coin and gold certificates declined, the amount of gold coin alone increased by nearly $120 million, from $65 million in April 1931 to $181 million in December 1932. That increase may have reflected a preference for gold coin in the earlier period, though to some extent it must reflect the growth of all forms of currency as opposed to deposits. But if it does reflect a preference for gold, that preference was not sufficiently widespread or dramatic to attract much attention. In February and March 1933, the situation was entirely different, as shown by the sharp spurt in gold coin and certificates in early 1933 in Chart 32A. Fears of devaluation were widespread and the the public's preference for gold was unmistakable. On February 23, 1933, Harrison told the directors of the New York Reserve Bank, "there is little that foreigners can do to hurt our gold position, . . . the real danger comes from domestic sources."[60]

---

[59] Gold certificates in circulation declined in all but three months in 1931 and 1932—when the certificates may have been paid out partly because of a shortage of other forms of currency, as in Feb. and Mar. 1933 before the bank holiday—for a net change of $460 million. Although there is no acknowledgment in the *Annual Report* for 1931 and 1932 that such a retirement policy was in effect, it is significant that the *Federal Reserve Bulletin* (Nov. 1931, p. 604) contains the following comment:

In considering the gold position of the country, it should be noted also that there are $1,000,000,000 of gold certificates in circulation, a large part of which can be retired by the Federal reserve banks by substituting an equivalent amount of Federal [reserve] notes. The retirement of gold certificates would increase the gold holdings of the reserve banks, and of this increase 40 per cent would be required as reserves against the additional Federal reserve notes and 60 per cent would be added to the system's excess reserves.

[60] He went on to say, "During the last ten days out-payments of gold coin at this bank, and, probably, at all of the Federal reserve banks have been heavier than in any recent similar period. This movement represents something more than the hoarding of currency, which reflects a distrust of banks; it represents in addition a distrust of the currency itself and it is inspired by talk of devaluation of the dollar and inflation of the currency" (Harrison, Notes, Vol. III).

Harrison made efforts to get banks to discourage hoarding. He suggested that they refuse to provide facilities for storage of gold and to grant loans against the collateral of an equivalent amount of gold. With respect to the first, he suggested that banks impose no obstacles to the acquisition of gold but make no offer of safekeeping facilities; with respect to the second, he advised banks to decline a loan to buy gold on the ground that it was a loan for a capital purpose. He said, "I saw no occasion for a member bank, in these times particularly when so many people who needed credit for business purposes could not obtain the credit, to make loans to their customers for the purpose of buying gold to hoard. It was nothing but a speculative loan gambling on our going off the gold standard" (Conversations, Vol. II, Feb. 9, 1933). Direct pressure had come full circle.

3. *Bank Failures*

The preceding account gives a prominent place in the sequence of events during the contraction to the successive waves of bank failures. Three questions about those failures deserve further attention: Why were the bank failures important? What was the origin of the bank failures? What was the attitude of the Federal Reserve System toward the bank failures?

ROLE OF BANK FAILURES

The bank failures had two different aspects. First, they involved capital losses to both their owners and their depositors, just as the failure of any other group of business enterprises involved losses to their owners and creditors. Second, given the policy followed by the Reserve System, the failures were the mechanism through which a drastic decline was produced in the stock of money. Which aspect was the more important for the course of business?

For the United States, the two aspects were so closely related that it may seem impossible to distinguish them and to judge their separate effects. But even for the United States alone, a few figures serve to show that the second was vastly more important than the first. Regarded solely in their first aspect, the failures imposed losses totaling about $2.5 billion on stockholders, depositors and other creditors of the more than 9,000 banks that suspended operations during the four years from 1930 through 1933. Slightly more than half the loss fell on depositors, the rest on other creditors and stockholders.[61] A loss of $2.5 billion is certainly sizable, yet by itself it would not entitle bank failures to the amount of attention we and other students of the period have devoted to them. By comparison, over the same four years, the value of all preferred and common stock in all enterprises in the United States is estimated to have declined by $85 billion. Or, to make a different comparison, the decline in the total value of all shares listed on the New York Stock Exchange in October 1929 is estimated to have been nearly $15½ billion.[62] As a fraction of total wealth, the losses produced by bank failures were minor and would deserve no more attention than losses of a comparable amount in, say, real estate.

---

[61] Loss to depositors, estimated at $1.3 billion (unpublished FDIC estimates; see source notes to Table 16, part 1); loss to other creditors is a rough guess; loss to stockholders, estimated at $0.9 billion (*Federal Reserve Bulletin*, Sept. 1937, p. 897). A sizable fraction of the losses was not realized until after the end of the banking holiday. Of the more than 9,000 banks that suspended in the years from 1930 through 1933, more than 3,500 suspended after Mar. 15, 1933.

[62] *Historical Statistics of the United States, Colonial Times to 1957,* Bureau of the Census, 1960, Series F-175, p. 150; *Business Statistics,* 1932 Supplement, p. 104.

In the second aspect, the situation is entirely different. The total stock of money fell by over one-third from 1929 to 1933; commercial bank deposits fell by over 42 per cent; in absolute amount, they fell $18 billion. Total deposits in suspended banks alone were much larger than losses, close to $7 billion in the same four years. If the bank failures deserve special attention, it is clearly because they were the mechanism through which the drastic decline in the stock of money was produced, and because the stock of money plays an important role in economic developments. The bank failures were important not primarily in their own right, but because of their indirect effect. If they had occurred to precisely the same extent without producing a drastic decline in the stock of money, they would have been notable but not crucial. If they had not occurred, but a correspondingly sharp decline had been produced in the stock of money by some other means, the contraction would have been at least equally severe and probably even more so.

Persuasive evidence for this final statement is provided by Canadian experience. Canada had no bank failures at all during the depression; its 10 banks with 3,000-odd branches throughout the country did not even experience any runs, although, presumably as a preventive measure, an eleventh chartered bank with a small number of branches was merged with a larger bank in May 1931. But because Canada kept its exchange rate with the United States fixed until Britain left the gold standard in September 1931 and then maintained its exchange rate at a new level involving a smaller depreciation than that undergone by the pound sterling, its internal level of income and its stock of money had to adjust to maintain external equilibrium. Though the required fall in both prices and income was sharp, the depreciation of the Canadian exchange rate permitted the percentage fall to be somewhat smaller than that in the United States. The stock of money fell sharply also, but by a much smaller percentage than in the United States. Even the smaller fall was, however, nearly one and a half times as large as the fall in any contraction in U.S. history since the Civil War except only the 1929–33 contraction. So it can hardly be regarded as minor. The relevant figures are as follows:[63]

Percentage Decline, 1929–33	*United States*	*Canada*
Stock of money	33	13
Net national product	53	49
Velocity	29	41

[63] Except for the Canadian currency component, which is an uncentered annual average of monthly data, money stock figures are annual averages of monthly data, centered on June 30. Canadian data are sums of demand, notice, and provincial government deposits in chartered banks, minus duplications (*Canada Gazette*, Dominion of Canada, Jan. 1929–Jan. 1934), plus currency held by the public (*Canada Year Book*, 1947, Dominion Bureau of Statistics, p. 1023). Net national income at factor cost, for Canada, from *Canadian Statistical Review*, 1953 Supplement, Dominion Bureau of Statistics, p. 15.

Why was the decline in the stock of money so much sharper in the United States relative to the decline in income than it was in Canada? Or, alternatively, why did not the stock of money in Canada have to fall much more sharply than it did to be consistent with so sharp a decline in income? The reason for the difference is, we believe, primarily the effect of the U.S. bank failures themselves. The bank failures made deposits a much less satisfactory form in which to hold assets than they had been before in the United States or than they remained in Canada. That, of course, is the reason they produced such a shift in the deposit-currency ratio in the United States. While currency was an alternative, it was not a fully satisfactory alternative, otherwise deposits would never have constituted so large a fraction of the total stock of money. Hence the demand for the sum of deposits and currency was reduced by the diminished attractiveness of deposits—an effect of the bank failures not heretofore considered. Of course, that effect was not strong enough to offset completely the increased demand for money relative to income as a result of the other factors associated with the contraction, such as the great increase in uncertainty, the decline in attractiveness of equities and real goods, and so on (see Chapter 12). If it had been, the amount of money would have fallen by a larger percentage than income fell, i.e., velocity would have risen rather than have fallen as it did. But the effect was strong enough to make the decline in velocity decidedly smaller in the United States than in Canada, where the same effect was not present. In Canada, deposits remained as attractive as they had ever been, and there was accordingly no reduction in the demand for money from this source. The other factors increasing the demand for money had full scope.

Paradoxically, therefore, the bank failures, by their effect on the demand for money, offset some of the harm they did by their effect on the supply of money. That is why we say that, if the same reduction in the stock of money had been produced in some other way, it would probably have involved an even larger fall in income than the catastrophic fall that did occur.

ORIGIN OF BANK FAILURES

The issue that has perhaps received the most attention centers on the reasons for the bank failures. Did they arise primarily from the financial practices of the preceding years? Or were they produced by the developments of the early thirties? Even if the first view were correct, the indirect monetary consequences of the failures are separable from the failures as such and need not have been also the near-inevitable consequences of the developments of the twenties. As we have just seen, it was the indirect consequences that were the most important effect of the bank failures.

As noted in Chapter 6, there is some evidence that the quality of loans and investments made by individuals, banks, and other financial institutions deteriorated in the late twenties relative to the early twenties in the ex ante sense that, had the later loans and investments been subject to the same economic environment as the earlier ones, they would have displayed a higher ratio of losses through default. The evidence for such deterioration is fully satisfactory only for foreign lending. For the rest, the studies made have not satisfactorily separated, and some have not even recognized, the difference between the ex ante deterioration, in the sense just specified, and the ex post deterioration that occurred because the loans and investments came to fruition and had to be repaid in the midst of a major depression. Loans and investments, identical in every respect except the year made, would have fared worse if made in the later than if made in the earlier twenties. By their concentration on ex post experience, authors of most of the studies unquestionably exaggerate whatever difference in ex ante quality there was. Indeed, many of the results are consistent with no deterioration at all in ex ante quality.

If the evidence is unsatisfactory for loans and investments in general, it is even sparser and more unsatisfactory for the loans and investments of commercial banks in particular. And there is some reason to believe that the experience of banks may have been different from that of other lenders. During the later years of the twenties, particularly in 1928 and 1929, banks were under steady reserve pressure. As we have seen, their total deposits were roughly constant from early 1928 to after the cyclical peak in August 1929. Whatever they might have done in the generally optimistic and exuberant environment of the time if they had been more plentifully supplied with reserves, they had no choice but to be highly selective in their loans and investments.

If there was any deterioration at all in the ex ante quality of loans and investments of banks, it must have been minor, to judge from the slowness with which it manifested itself. As we have seen, the contraction in business during the first fourteen months from the peak in August 1929 to October 1930 and particularly during the twelve months after the stock market crash was extremely severe. One reason may have been that banks were being forced to contract by a reduction in high-powered money, so that their deposits fell by 2 per cent in the course of the fourteen months. Yet, in that fourteen-month period, deposits in banks that suspended operations were only one-fifth to one-third higher than they were in the fourteen months beginning with either the cyclical peak of May 1923 or of October 1926: the amounts are $263 million for 1923–24, $281 million for 1926–27, and $347 million for 1929–30. In both earlier contractions, the decline in general economic activity, and hence the pressure on borrowers, was milder than from 1929 to 1930;

and, in addition, deposits in commercial banks rose by 5 to 6 per cent rather than falling as they did from 1929 to 1930.

The great surge in bank failures that characterized the first banking crisis after October 1930 may possibly have resulted from poor loans and investments made in the twenties. After the failure of the Bank of United States in December 1930, Governor Harrison told his board of directors that "the Reserve Bank had been working for a year or more to improve conditions in the Bank of United States, although there was no evidence that the condition of the bank was impaired," and J. H. Case, chairman of the board, said the bank's condition was probably not satisfactory in July 1929.[64] However, the subsequent pay-out record during the liquidation of the Bank of United States suggests that, if there was any permanent impairment of assets at the time the bank failed, it could not have been great.

Whatever may have been true of the initial bank failures in the first banking crisis, any ex ante deterioration in the quality of loans and investments in the later twenties or simply the acquisition of low-quality loans and investments in that period, even if no different in quality than in earlier periods, was a minor factor in the subsequent bank failures. As we have seen, the banking system as a whole was in a position to meet the demands of depositors for currency only by a multiple contraction of deposits, hence of assets. Under such circumstances, any runs on banks for whatever reason became to some extent self-justifying, whatever the quality of assets held by banks. Banks had to dump their assets on the market, which inevitably forced a decline in the market value of those assets and hence of the remaining assets they held. The impairment in the market value of assets held by banks, particularly in their bond portfolios, was the most important source of impairment of capital leading to bank suspensions,[65] rather than the default of specific loans or of specific bond issues.[65] As W. R. Burgess, at the time a deputy governor of the

[64] Harrison, Notes, Vol. I, Dec. 18, 1930.

[65] The president of Federation Bank and Trust Company, closed by the New York State Superintendent of Banks on Oct. 30, 1931, explained that the bank had prospered for many years "and as a matter of fact right up to the past few months, when due to the nationwide rapid and unforeseen depreciation in bonds and other securities, the falling away in values of the bonds and securities owned by the company impaired the bank's capital structure" (*Commercial and Financial Chronicle,* Nov. 7, 1931, p. 3038).

In his contemporary account of the American banking system, R. W. Goldsmith wrote: "The depression of bond values, which started as far back as 1929 in the field of urban real estate bonds and reached foreign bonds and land bank bonds in the course of 1931, began to endanger the whole banking structure and notably the large city banks the moment first-grade bonds were affected in a most drastic way: From the middle of 1931 to the middle of 1932, railroad bonds lost nearly 36 per cent of their market value, public utility bonds 27 per cent, industrial bonds 22 per cent, foreign bonds 45 per cent, and even United States Government securities 10 per cent" (R. W. Goldschmidt [Goldsmith], *The Changing Structure*

New York Reserve Bank, told the Bank's board of directors in February 1931, the chief problem confronting many banks was the severe depreciation in their bond accounts; "given a better bond market and rising bond prices, . . . the condition of banks now jeopardized by depreciation in their bond accounts would, in many cases, improve automatically beyond the point of immediate danger."[66] Because there was an active market for bonds and continuous quotation of their prices, a bank's capital was more likely to be impaired, in the judgment of bank examiners, when it held bonds that were expected to be and were honored in full when due than when it held bonds for which there was no good market and few quotations. So long as the latter did not come due, they were likely to be carried on the books at face value; only actual defaults or postponements of payment would reduce the examiners' evaluation. Paradoxically, therefore, assets regarded by the banks as particularly liquid and as providing them with a secondary reserve turned out to offer the most serious threat to their solvency.

The most extreme example of the process we have been describing is the experience after Britain left the gold standard. The decline of 10 per cent in the price of government bonds and of 20 per cent in the price of high-grade corporate bonds (noted in the preliminary memorandum for the January 11, 1932, meeting of the Open Market Policy Conference, cited earlier) clearly did not reflect any deterioration in the quality of credit in the twenties or "bad" banking in any meaningful sense of the term. It reflected the inevitable effect of the enforced dumping of bonds by banks to reduce the volume of their assets by a large multiple of the amount of additional currency supplied to depositors.

If deterioration of credit quality or bad banking was the trigger, which it may to some extent have been, the damaging bullet it discharged was the inability of the banking system to acquire additional high-powered money to meet the resulting demands of depositors for currency, without a multiple contraction of deposits. That inability was responsible alike for the extent and importance of bank failures and for the indirect effect bank failures had on the stock of money. In the absence of the provision of additional high-powered money, banks that suffered runs as a result

---

of *American Banking,* London, Routledge, 1933, p. 106). We are indebted to Manuel Gottlieb for this reference.

Commenting on bank suspensions in 1932, Bray Hammond wrote: "The situation had worked to the point where the stronger banks were being dragged down by the weaker banks, partly because the latter drew on the former for reserves and partly because the forced liquidation of portfolios by banks in difficulties impaired the value of portfolios of all other banks" ("Historical Introduction," *Banking Studies,* Board of Governors of the Federal Reserve System, 1941, p. 29).

[66] Harrison, Notes, Vol. I, Feb. 26, 1931. See also footnote 12, above.

of the initial failure of "bad" banks would not have been helped by holding solely U.S. government securities in addition to required reserves. If the composition of their assets did not stop the runs simply by its effect on depositors' confidence, the banks would still have had to dump their government securities on the market to acquire needed high-powered money, and many would have failed.[67] Alternatively, the composition of assets held by banks would hardly have mattered if additional high-powered money had been made available from whatever source to meet the demands of depositors for currency without requiring a multiple contraction of deposits and assets. The trigger would have discharged only a blank cartridge. The banks would have been under no necessity to dump their assets. There would have been no major decline in the market prices of the assets and no impairment in the capital accounts of banks. The failure of a few bad banks would not have caused the insolvency of many other banks any more than during the twenties when a large number of banks failed. And even if an abnormally large number of banks had failed because they were bad, imposing losses on depositors, other creditors, and stockholders, comparable to those actually imposed, that would have been only a regrettable occurrence and not a catastrophe if it had not been accompanied by a major decline in the stock of money.

FEDERAL RESERVE SYSTEM'S ATTITUDE

The failure of the Bank of United States provoked much soul searching by the directors of the New York Reserve Bank. They devoted meeting after meeting from mid-December 1930 to April 1931 to discussions of the responsibilities of the Reserve Bank with respect to member bank suspensions and of the actions it could take to prevent them. They were well aware of the serious shock the failures had administered to confidence not only in commercial banks but also in the Federal Reserve System. Owen D. Young, then deputy chairman of the board of directors of the New York Bank, repeated to his fellow directors the remark of an upstate New York banker that the failure of the Bank of United States "had shaken confidence in the Federal Reserve System more than any other occurrence in recent years."[68] At the first joint meeting of the Federal Reserve Board and the Open Market Policy Conference after the banking difficulties had developed, Adolph Miller, a member of the Board, commented that "the banking situation was now more important than the credit situa-

[67] Of course, had banks held only U.S. government securities in addition to their required reserves, the Reserve System would have been under much greater pressure than it was to intervene by providing additional high-powered money to support the prices of those securities. But that is an aspect of the problem wholly different from the effect of the possible deterioration of credit quality.

[68] Harrison, Notes, Vol. II, Aug. 13, 1931.

tion, and asked what the governors were planning to do in different districts if further banking trouble started."[69] The minutes of directors' meetings of the New York Bank and memoranda prepared for meetings of the Open Market Policy Conference reveal that the technical personnel of the Bank and the Board were fully aware of the interconnection between the banking and the credit situations, and of the effects of the liquidation of securities to meet the demands of depositors.[70] Repeatedly during the next two years, the problem of bank failures and bank supervision was discussed at meetings within the System.

Despite the attention to the problem after 1930, the only System actions directed specifically at the problem of bank failures were the proposals noted above for measures that others might take, with particular emphasis on proposals designed to permit assets to be valued more liberally in bank examinations. The general tenor of System comments, both inside and out, was defensive, stressing that bank failures were a problem of bank management which was not the System's responsibility.

The major reason the System was so belated in showing concern about bank failures and so inactive in responding to them was undoubtedly limited understanding of the connection between bank failures, runs on banks, contraction of deposits, and weakness of the bond markets—connections we have tried to spell out earlier in this chapter. The technical personnel of the New York Bank understood these connections, as undoubtedly many other individuals in the System did also; but most of the governors of the Banks, members of the Board, and other administrative officials of the System did not. They tended to regard bank failures as regrettable consequences of bad management and bad banking practices, or as inevitable reactions to prior speculative excesses, or as a consequence but hardly a cause of the financial and economic collapse in process. As implied in Miller's comment quoted above, they regarded the banking situation as something different from the credit situation.

Four additional circumstances may help to explain the System's failure both to develop concern over bank closings at an earlier date and to undertake more positive measures when concern did develop. (1) Federal Reserve officials had no feeling of responsibility for nonmember banks. In 1921–29 and the first ten months of 1930, most failed banks were nonmembers, and nonmembers held a high percentage of the deposits involved. (2) The failures for that period were concentrated among smaller banks and, since the most influential figures in the System were big-city bankers who deplored the existence of smaller banks, their disappearance may have been viewed with complacency. (3) Even in November and December 1930, when the number of failures increased sharply, over 80

[69] Harrison, Open Market, Vol. II, minutes of meeting, Jan. 21, 1931, p. 7.
[70] See, for example, quotations in footnote 12, above.

per cent were nonmembers. (4) The relatively few large member banks that failed at the end of 1930 were regarded by many Reserve officials as unfortunate cases of bad management and therefore not subject to correction by central bank action.[71]

In September 1931, when Governor Harrison convened a meeting of commercial bankers to discuss means of making deposits in closed banks available, he recalled that "at one time it was the feeling of many of us down town that the effects of the failure of . . . small banks in the community could be isolated," but "it was clear that the continued closing of institutions in the city is now having serious repercussions. . . ."[72]

4. *International Character of the Contraction*

In 1929, most countries of the Western world had returned to a monetary standard involving fixed exchange rates between different national currencies. The standard was widely known as the gold-exchange standard because many countries kept their monetary reserves in the form of balances of other currencies convertible into gold at fixed prices, notably sterling and dollars, rather than in the form of gold itself. Official agencies in such countries, usually the central banks, often fixed exchange rates directly by standing ready to buy or sell the national currency at fixed rates in terms of other currencies, rather than indirectly by standing ready to buy or sell gold at fixed prices in terms of the national currency.

Since the gold-exchange standard, like the gold standard, involved fixed exchange rates, it also meant that, so long as the standard was maintained, prices and incomes in different countries were intimately connected. They had to behave so as to preserve a rough equilibrium in the balance of payments among the countries. The use of the gold-exchange standard did mean, however, that there was less leeway in the adjustments among countries—the rough equilibrium could not be quite so rough as under the full gold standard. The gold-exchange standard rendered the international financial system more vulnerable to disturbances for the same reason that the rise in the deposit-reserve ratio rendered the domestic monetary system more vulnerable: because it raised the ratio of claims on the relevant high-powered money—in this case, ultimately, gold—to the amount of high-powered money available to meet those claims.

The links forged by the fixed rates of exchange ensured a worldwide decline in income and prices after 1929, just as the links forged by the less rigidly fixed exchange rates in 1920 ensured a worldwide decline then. No major contraction involving a substantial fall in prices could develop in any one country without those links enforcing its trans-

[71] We are indebted to Clark Warburton for this paragraph.
[72] Harrison, Office, Vol. II, Sept. 11, 1931.

mission and spread to other countries. There was sufficient play in the links to permit minor uncoordinated movements but not to permit major ones.

As in 1920, the worldwide scope of the contraction once it got under way does not mean that it did not originate in the United States. Ever since World War I at the latest, the United States has been a sufficiently important participant in world trade and in world capital and financial markets and has held a sufficiently large fraction of the world's gold stock to be capable of initiating worldwide movements and not merely of reacting to them. Of course, if it did initiate a worldwide disturbance, it would inevitably be affected in turn by reflex influences from the rest of the world.

We saw in Chapter 5 that there is good reason to regard the 1920–21 contraction as having been initiated primarily in the United States. The initial step—the sharp rise in discount rates in January 1920—was indeed a consequence of the prior gold outflow, but that in turn reflected the United States inflation in 1919. The rise in discount rates produced a reversal of the gold movement in May. The second step—the rise in discount rates in June 1920 to the highest level in Federal Reserve history before or since—was a deliberate act of policy involving a reaction stronger than was needed, since a gold inflow had already begun. It was succeeded by a heavy gold inflow, proof positive that the other countries were being forced to adapt to United States action in order to check their loss of gold, rather than the reverse.

The situation in 1929 was not dissimilar. Again, the initial climactic event—the stock market crash—occurred in the United States. The series of developments which started the stock of money on its accelerated downward course in late 1930 was again predominantly domestic in origin. It would be difficult indeed to attribute the sequence of bank failures to any major current influence from abroad. And again, the clinching evidence that the United States was in the van of the movement and not a follower is the flow of gold. If declines elsewhere were being transmitted to the United States, the transmission mechanism would be a balance of payments deficit in the United States as a result of a decline in prices and incomes elsewhere relative to prices and incomes in the United States. That decline would lead to a gold outflow from the United States which, in turn, would tend—if the United States followed gold-standard rules—to lower the stock of money and thereby income and prices in the United States. However, the U.S. gold stock rose during the first two years of the contraction and did not decline, demonstrating as in 1920 that other countries were being forced to adapt to our monetary policies rather than the reverse.

The international effects were severe and the transmission rapid, not only because the gold-exchange standard had rendered the international financial system more vulnerable to disturbances, but also because the United States did not follow gold-standard rules. We did not permit the inflow of gold to expand the U.S. money stock. We not only sterilized it, we went much further. Our money stock moved perversely, going down as the gold stock went up. In August 1929, our money stock was 10.6 times our gold stock; by August 1931, it was 8.3 times the gold stock. The result was that other countries not only had to bear the whole burden of adjustment but also were faced with continued additional disturbances in the same direction, to which they had to adjust. As Harrison noted in early 1931, foreign commentators were particularly critical of the monetary policy of the United States because

> the gold as it came into the country has been used by member banks to repay Federal reserve credit in one form or another, with the result that in this period the total volume of Federal reserve credit had declined by an amount equal to the gold imports. Thus it may be said that the United States has prevented the usual or normal effect of gold which has come to it . . . . The evils to the world of continued gold sterilization . . . are so great as to make desirable a careful scrutiny of Federal reserve open market policy.[73]

The effects first became severe in those countries that had returned to gold with the smallest actual gold reserves, and whose financial structures had been most seriously weakened by World War I—Austria, Germany, Hungary, and Rumania. To shore up the financial systems of those countries, international loans, in which the Reserve System participated, were arranged. But so long as either the basic pressure on those countries deriving from deflation in the United States was not relieved, or the fixed exchange-rate link which bound them to the U.S. dollar was not severed, such assistance was at best a temporary palliative. In country after country, that is what it proved to be. As they experienced financial difficulties, the United States, as we have seen, was in turn affected by the reflex influence of the events it had set in train.

The key role of fixed exchange rates in the international transmission mechanism is cogently illustrated by the case of China. China was on a silver rather than a gold standard. As a result, it had the equivalent of a floating exchange rate with respect to gold-standard countries. A decline in the gold price of silver had the same effect as a depreciation in the foreign exchange value of the Chinese yuan. The effect was to insulate Chinese internal economic conditions from the worldwide depression. As world prices fell in terms of gold, so did the gold price of silver. Hence the prices of goods in terms of silver could remain approximately the same. China could continue to maintain external balance without undergoing an internal deflation. And that is what happened. From 1929

[73] Harrison, Open Market, Vol. II, Apr. 27, 1931.

to 1931, China was hardly affected internally by the holocaust that was sweeping the gold-standard world,[74] just as in 1920–21, Germany had been insulated by her hyperinflation and associated floating exchange rate.[75]

The first major country to cut the link was Britain, when she left the gold standard in 1931. The trough of the depression in Britain and in other countries that accompanied Britain in leaving gold was reached in the third quarter of 1932. In the countries that remained on the gold standard or, like Canada, that went only part way with Britain, the depression dragged on. In China, whose currency appreciated relative to the pound as a result of the sharp depreciation of the pound relative to gold, the depression set in for the first time in 1931.

Of course, the country in the vanguard of such an international movement need not stay there. France, which had accumulated a large stock of gold as a result of returning to the gold standard in 1928 at an exchange rate that undervalued the franc, and therefore had much leeway, at some point passed the United States and not only began to add to its gold stock but also, after late 1931, to drain gold from the United States. The link between the franc and the dollar was cut when the United States suspended gold payments in March 1933, which proved to be the business cycle trough for the United States and countries closely linked to it. In France, which stayed on gold for a further interval, the contraction dragged on still longer. Although there was an upturn from July 1932 to July 1933, the low point of the interwar years was not reached until April 1935.

5. *Development of Monetary Policy*

The course of monetary policy in the difficult and critical years of the contraction was greatly influenced by the struggle for power within the Federal Reserve System, the beginnings of which were described in the preceding chapter. At the time of the stock market crash, the New York Reserve Bank acted in the tradition of its earlier dominance, moving rapidly, decisively, and on its own. The adverse reaction of the Board greatly inhibited further independent measures by New York.

In 1930, New York strongly favored expansionary open market operations, but after the middle of the year was unable to persuade either the other Bank governors—all of whom by this time had become members of the reorganized Open Market Policy Conference, which replaced the earlier Open Market Investment Committee—or the Board in Washington. The same was true in 1931, except that New York was less

[74]Arthur Salter, *China and Silver,* New York, Economic Forum, 1934, pp. 3–6, 15–17.

[75] Frank D. Graham, *Exchange, Prices, and Production in Hyperinflation: Germany, 1920–23,* Princeton University Press, 1931, pp. 287–288.

vigorous in pressing for expansionary action, though it was now supported by the new governor (Eugene Meyer) of the Federal Reserve Board.

The reaction to Britain's departure from gold did not provoke a flare-up of those conflicts. The measures adopted at that time were favored by almost all affiliated with the System. The agreement reflected the dominant importance then attached to the preservation of the gold standard and the greater significance attached to external than to internal stability, by both the System and the community at large. Not long after, the differences within the System that had been submerged in the fall of 1931 re-emerged, New York generally pressing for expansionary open market operations, supported by the governor and some other members of the Board and by a few Bank governors, and opposed by most of the Bank governors.

The open market operation of 1932 was acceded to largely under Congressional pressure and with the new Glass-Steagall Act ostensibly permitting release of the System's expansionary powers. The operation was terminated in August, shortly after Congress adjourned, because so many Bank governors remained unenthusiastic about the policy and reluctant or unwilling to pursue it. The deadlock persisted through the rest of the contraction.

THE STOCK MARKET CRASH, OCTOBER 1929

At the time of the stock market crash, the Open Market Investment Committee consisted of five Bank governors with the New York governor as chairman. It was operating under its recommendation to the Board, September 4, which had been approved by the Board on October 1, to purchase "not to exceed $25,000,000 a week" of short-term government securities if needed to supplement purchases of acceptances, "for the purpose of avoiding any increase and, if possible, facilitating some further reduction in the total volume of member bank discounts . . . ." Up to the week ending October 23, the Committee had not made any government security purchases because bills had been available. The System's holdings had declined by $16 million, while its bill holdings had increased by $115 million.[76]

When the crash came, the New York Bank had no doubt about what steps should be taken and proceeded to take them. It purchased $160 million of government securities in addition to encouraging New York banks to discount freely. The amount purchased was far in excess of the amount that the Open Market Investment Committee was authorized to purchase, but the New York Bank did not claim to be operating for the Committee. It contended it had the right to purchase government secu-

[76] Harrison, Open Market, Vol. I, minutes, Sept. 24, 1929, and letter, dated Oct. 1, 1929, Young to Harrison.

rities for its own account, as a matter of general credit policy, without the Board's approval.[77] Harrison informed Governor Young of the Federal Reserve Board that his directors had authorized him to purchase government securities without limitation as to amount, and that on October 29, before the call loan rate was announced, a purchase had been arranged.

Members of the Board regarded the New York Bank's failure to seek the authorization of the Board before taking action as smacking of insubordination, though some regarded the action itself as desirable. As a legal matter, the New York Bank seemed clearly within its rights. Under the 1923 agreement setting up the Open Market Investment Committee, each Reserve Bank retained the right to purchase and hold government securities for its own account. Young and most Board members acknowledged the legal right yet felt that the challenge to the Board's authority was insupportable. After much discussion, the Board finally authorized Young to tell Harrison that, if New York should request approval of a reduction of its rate to 5 per cent, the Board would consent on condition that no further purchases of government securities be made except with approval of the Board.[78] On November 1, the discount rate at the New York Bank was so reduced. To the New York directors it was clear that the System ought to proceed immediately with further purchases for "unless this is done, after the events of the past weeks, there may be greater danger of a recession in business with consequent depression and unemployment, which we should do all in our power to prevent," as they declared in a resolution they adopted on November 7.[79] Under the leadership of Harrison, the Open Market Investment Committee, meeting November 12, recommended that "the present limit of $25,000,000 per week on the purchase of government securities be removed and that the Committee be authorized in lieu thereof to purchase not to exceed $200,000,000 of government securities for account of such banks as care to participate . . . ," having in mind also the fact "that present conditions may possibly develop to the point where, as an emergency measure, in the interest of maintaining banking and business stability, it may be necessary quickly to purchase large amounts of Government securities in order to avoid any undue stringency in credit."[80]

[77] Of the $160 million government securities purchased by New York in the week ending Oct. 30, $75 million was transferred to System account. During the following two weeks, the New York Bank bought an additional $25 million directly for System account.

[78] Hamlin, Diary, Vol. 16, Oct. 29, 30, 1929, pp. 187–196. Miller did not consider the purchase desirable. He suggested a resolution to the effect that the Board would not have approved the purchase, had it been consulted; that New York was more concerned about the stock market than the general credit situation; that forcing the banks to come to the discount window would have been the proper response.

[79] For the resolution, see Harrison, Miscellaneous, Vol. I.

[80] Open Market, Vol. I, minutes of meeting, Nov. 12, 1929.

The next day, the Board notified the Committee that "the general situation was not sufficiently clarified for the System to formulate and adopt a permanent open market policy at that time," but conceded that if "an emergency should arise with such suddenness and be so acute that it is not practicable to confer with the Governor, the Board will interpose no objection to a purchase operation being undertaken, with the understanding, however, that prompt advice of such purchase be furnished the Board."[81]

On November 15, Governor Young of the Federal Reserve Board was in New York, and Harrison had an exchange of views with him: "I told him," Harrison wrote in recording the interview, "that I wanted a very frank and complete conversation with him regarding our present differences in the matter of the purchase of government securities . . . that it had become obvious that the Federal Reserve Board and the directors of the Federal Reserve Bank of New York were reaching a point in their views regarding their respective powers where it might have very serious consequences unless we could come to some sort of a workable understanding or agreement . . . I told him that more and more the Board had taken to itself not supervisory powers but the equivalent of operating functions and the responsibility for the detailed transactions of the various Federal reserve banks. . . ." Harrison then reviewed the Board's veto, earlier in 1929 for a period of four months, of the increase in the discount rate the directors of the New York Bank had repeatedly voted; the Board's decision that year to fix the spread above the minimum buying rate for acceptances within which the Bank might operate, although it had never done so earlier, and, during the fall of the year, its actual determination of the minimum rate, which had always been the Bank's prerogative; and finally, its stand

that we should go to the Federal Reserve Board in advance for a prior approval of any transactions in government securities . . . I told him that the logical consequence of his point of view, which was that the Federal Reserve Board should approve of all these things in advance, was that the Federal Reserve Board would become a central bank operating in Washington . . . [H]is only comment was that the Federal Reserve Board had been given most extraordinarily wide powers, that as long as the Board had those powers, they would feel free to exercise them and Congress could determine whether they objected to having a central bank operating in Washington.[82]

Neither side was prepared to make any concessions until Governor Young had a meeting with Owen D. Young, deputy chairman of the board of directors of the New York Bank, in the office of Secretary of the Treasury Mellon, the ex-officio chairman of the Reserve Board, on November 22 to discuss the Board's power over transactions in govern-

[81] *Ibid.*, letter, dated Nov. 13, 1929, Young to Harrison.
[82] Harrison, Conversations, Vol. I, Nov. 15, 1929.

ment securities. Secretary Mellon said he was willing to give the New York directors the widest discretion, but he realized that the Board had rights and duties in the matter. Owen D. Young said he saw no reason—apart from sudden critical emergencies, about which there was no dispute—his directors could not obtain the consent of the Board to all major transactions. Governor Young replied that was just what the Board wanted.[83]

The next day, November 23, Governor Young and Secretary Mellon met with Harrison, who stated that "we in New York were willing and prepared to operate any policy agreed upon either for our own account or for the System account." Young answered that he was prepared to approve without reservation the Open Market Investment Committee's recommendation of November 12, but first wanted to know

> where this would leave the debated question of the New York bank's operating for its own account. I [Harrison] told him that I felt that this involved a matter of procedure and jurisdiction which I would like to leave for determination sometime later on when we were through this critical period and when we could work out some mutually satisfactory procedure when conditions and peoples' emotions were in a quieter and more normal state. I then made this proposition: That if the Federal Reserve Board would approve the Open Market Investment Committee's report without qualification, leaving it to the committee to execute, I would recommend to our directors on next Wednesday [November 27] that the Federal Reserve Bank of New York refrain, until such time as it and the Federal Reserve Board might formulate some mutually satisfactory procedure, from purchasing government securities for its own account as a matter of general credit policy without the Board's approval.

As a result of this understanding, the Board reconsidered, November 25, and voted to approve the Committee's recommendation and the policy outlined in the resolution of the directors of the New York Bank.[84] Although authorized to purchase $200 million, the Committee purchased only $155 million between November 27, 1929, and January 1, 1930.

In response to inquiries from other Banks about the New York purchases during the week of the stock market crash, Harrison wrote a long letter to all governors on November 27, describing the situation in New York at the time, explaining the reasons for the measures the Bank took, and defending them. Some governors supported the action and ex-

[83] Hamlin, Diary, Vol. 17, Nov. 12, 13, 22, 1929, pp. 13, 17, 20–22, 31–32.

[84] The motion to approve was passed 5 to 3, the Secretary of the Treasury and the Comptroller voting with Governor Young, Vice-Governor Platt, and Hamlin. Miller objected on the ground that "money was now cheap and would be made cheaper by the purchase of Government securities" and that it would be bad Federal Reserve policy—"abdication in favor of the Federal Reserve Bank of New York." The two other negative votes were cast by Board members Edward Cunningham, an Iowa farmer, and George James, a Memphis merchant (see section 7, below). Harrison, Miscellaneous, Vol. I, letter, dated Nov. 25, 1929, Young to Harrison; Office, Vol. II, memorandum of Nov. 25, 1929; Hamlin, Diary, Vol. 17, Nov. 24, 25, 1929, pp. 35–36, 38–40.

pressed willingness to participate in the purchases. Others criticized the action on the ground that it merely delayed "natural liquidation" and hence recovery.[85]

The situation which confronted the New York Bank during the first few weeks after the crash was to recur during the succeeding years of the contraction: it had a policy, which the Board or the other Banks would not approve, or would approve only reluctantly after protracted discussion. At the time of the crash, New York went ahead on its own. Though the Bank then yielded to the Board in November 1929, later on it again considered but, as we shall see, did not adopt, the alternative of ignoring the System account and purchasing for its own account, as it had in October 1929.

FROM THE STOCK MARKET CRASH TO BRITAIN'S
DEPARTURE FROM GOLD, 1929–31

From the time of the crash on, the New York Bank favored the reduction of discount rates and purchase of bills and securities in sufficiently large amounts to offset reductions in discounts. The directors of the New York Bank apparently voted to reduce the discount rate from 5 per cent to 4½ per cent for the first time on November 14, 1929, and the Board gave its approval. On January 30, 1930, the directors voted to reduce the rate to 4 per cent; the Board disapproved by a tie vote. On February 7, the reduction was again voted by the directors and on the first vote by the Board again lost on a tie vote. One member then changed his vote to affirmative, not because he approved the rate reduction, but because he disapproved defeat of a motion on a tie vote; so the reduction was approved. The reduction of the rate to 3½ per cent on March 14 was apparently approved by the Board the first time the directors voted it. On April 24, the directors voted to reduce the discount rate to 3 per cent; the reduction was disapproved by the Board. It was voted again on May 1, with the directors this time even considering but deciding against a public statement if the Board should again disapprove. However, the Board approved it. Similar repeated delays were encountered in getting Board approval of reductions in buying rates on bills.[86]

[85] Harrison, Miscellaneous, Vol. I, Nov. 27, 1929; for criticism, see Notes, Vol. I, meeting of executive committee, June 9, 1930.
[86] For the time before Apr. 17, 1930, the first date of minutes of directors' meetings of the New York Reserve Bank in the Harrison Papers, we have relied mainly on Hamlin's Diary for statements about delays in Board approval of New York's requests for reductions in discount rates. Hamlin simply notes the Board's approval on Nov. 14, 1929, without indicating whether the motion to reduce was before the Board for the first time. He does not refer to the reduction in the rate, effective Mar. 14, 1930. (See Hamlin, Diary, Vol. 17, Nov. 14, 1929; Jan. 30, Feb. 6, Apr. 24, May 1, 1930, pp. 23, 87, 97, 139–141, 145–146; also Harrison, Miscellaneous, Vol. I, letter, dated Feb. 5, 1930, Harrison to all governors; another letter,

New York had even less success in winning approval of its recommendations for open market purchases. After the purchases in the final months of 1929, which were in accord with the usual seasonal pattern of increase in Federal Reserve credit outstanding, the Open Market Investment Committee was most reluctant to engage in further purchases. Some members were in favor of selling government securities in the usual pattern of the post-Christmas season. The final recommendation of the January meeting of the Committee was that "no open market operations in Government securities [were] necessary at this time either to halt or to expedite the present trend of credit."[87]

In early March, concerned about the worsening of the economic situation and the inability of the New York Bank to maintain its bill portfolio, the directors of the Bank voted to authorize purchase of $50 million of government securities. The purchases were carried out after approval by the Board and a circular letter to all Bank governors asking whether they wanted to participate. When the Open Market Committee met formally at the end of March, it concluded that "at present there is no occasion for further purchases of Government securities."[88]

That was the final meeting of the Open Market Investment Committee. It was replaced by the Open Market Policy Conference of all twelve Bank governors, with an executive committee consisting initially of the same five governors who had constituted the Committee (New York, Boston, Chicago, Cleveland, Philadelphia). But the executive committee was in a different position from the former Committee. It was entrusted with executing policy decisions of the Conference; it did not, like the earlier Committee, both initiate and execute policy. The Conference itself remained a voluntary organization of equals. Each Bank was free to decide whether it would or would not participate in a purchase or sale recommended by the Conference, though dissenters were required to acquaint the Federal Reserve Board and the chairman of the executive committee with the reasons for not participating. Each Bank also reserved the option to withdraw from the Conference. New York was not at all happy about the change and consented to it reluctantly and only with the explicit proviso that the Conference had no authority over transactions in

---

dated Mar. 17, 1930, Case to Governor Young; and a letter, dated Apr. 29, 1930, Harrison to Platt; Notes, Vol. I, Apr. 24, May 1, 1930.)

At the Open Market Policy Conference meeting on May 21–22, 1930, Governor Harrison reported that "in a number of recent weeks the Federal Reserve Board had failed to approve without delay applications of the Federal Reserve Bank of New York for a lower minimum buying rate on bills, and that for considerable periods the New York bank had therefore been without any downward flexibility in its bill buying rate as was the case at that very time" (Open Market, Vol. I).

[87] *Ibid.*, minutes of meeting, Jan. 28–29, 1930.

[88] Miscellaneous, Vol. I, letter, dated Mar. 7, 1930, Case to all governors; Open Market, Vol. I, minutes of meeting, Mar. 24–25, 1930.

bankers' acceptances.[89] As in 1929, New York hoped to be able to accomplish through the purchase of bills what it might not be able to persuade the rest of the System to do through transactions in government securities. Unfortunately, New York was not successful with its alternative.

At its first meeting in May 1930, the Open Market Policy Conference made no recommendation but left limited authority in the hands of the executive committee. Early in June, Harrison recommended that the System undertake the purchase of $25 million a week for a two-week trial period, arguing that "small purchases of Government securities at this time could do no harm . . . and might be desirable," and, as in earlier years, suggesting that security purchases be resorted to only if easing through the acceptance market failed. The recommendation to purchase was much milder than the statements at the meetings of the New York directors, and the amount recommended was much smaller than they thought desirable. Indeed, "there was some reluctance" on the part of the New York directors "to accept this program on the grounds that our difficulties of credit administration have grown largely out of our disposition to postpone action and to administer remedies in homeopathic doses." Apparently, however, Harrison felt that a bold program was certain to be rejected and preferred agreement on a small program to rejection of a large one. A majority of the executive committee and of governors agreed (after being consulted by telephone or telegram), the Board approved, and the purchase was made. A decline in the System's bill holdings during the two weeks largely offset the effect of the purchase of government securities, so, on June 23, Harrison suggested that purchases continue in the amount of about $25 million a week. This time, the executive committee rejected the recommendation by a vote of 4 to 1.[90]

Faced with a clear rejection of its leadership, the New York Bank considered three alternatives: (1) simply to accede without further action in the hope that its views would eventually prevail; (2) to "withdraw from the . . . Conference and, assuming that the approval of the Federal Reserve Board either can be or need not be secured, purchase Government securities for the account of this bank"; (3) to conduct a campaign of persuasion. The Bank adopted the third alternative, perhaps partly because Harrison had lingering doubts about the validity of New York's

[89] Commenting the following year on the change, Harrison was recorded by Hamlin as saying that "he had always felt it was a mistake to put all the Governors on the Open Market Policy Conference; that the Governors came instructed by their directors; that under the former System the Executive Committee were never so instructed" (Hamlin, Diary, Vol. 19, Aug. 1931, p. 123). See also Harrison, Open Market, Vol. I, minutes of meeting, Mar. 24–25, 1930; Notes, Vol. I, May 1, 1930; Open Market, Vol. I, letter, dated May 15, 1930, Case to Young.

[90] Harrison, Open Market, Vol. I, minutes of meeting, May 21–22, 1930; Miscellaneous, Vol. I, telegram, dated June 3, 1930, Harrison to Young; Notes, Vol. I, June 5, 1930; Open Market, Vol. I, June 23, 1930.

position. As the report on the relevant directors' meeting has it, the decision to adopt the third alternative was influenced by the existence of a "real difference of opinion among those deemed capable of forming a judgment, as to the power of cheap and abundant credit, alone, to bring about improvement in business and in commodity prices."[91]

In July 1930, Harrison accordingly wrote a long letter to all governors, telling them his directors "felt so earnestly the need of continuing purchases of government securities that they have suggested that I write to you outlining some of the reasons why the Federal Reserve Bank of New York has for so many months favored having the Federal Reserve System do everything possible and within its power to facilitate a recovery of business." There followed a closely reasoned, informed, and well documented analysis of the economic situation and the problem of monetary policy. Harrison stressed the seriousness of the recession, indicated that while there were many other causes of the recession, tight money of the preceding two years had contributed to it, and placed greatest importance on the depressed state of the bond market and the limited availability of funds for long-term financing. "In previous business depressions," he wrote, "recovery has never taken place until there has been a strong bond market." Harrison acknowledged that there was little demand for short-term funds, and that "when the System buys securities, short-time money becomes more plentiful and cheaper." However, "it has been demonstrated in the past that in such circumstances, through a further increase in the reserves of member banks money will be made available for the bond market or shifted to the bond market from the short time market or from other investments less profitable than bonds." He pointed out that Federal Reserve credit had declined and that banks were sensitive to borrowing. "[A]n even small amount of borrowing under present conditions is as effective a restraint as substantially a greater amount was a year ago." He concluded that "while there may be no definite assurance that open market operations in government securities will of themselves promote any immediate recovery, we cannot foresee any appreciable harm that can result from such a policy and believe that the seriousness of the present depression is so great as to justify taking every possible step to facilitate improvement."[92]

One notable omission from Harrison's letter was reference to the stock of money, as such. Like almost every other document on monetary policy

[91] Harrison, Notes, Vol. I, June 26, 1930. On several occasions, Harrison revealed doubts (Notes, Vol. I, July 17, Sept. 17, 1930). It is clear from internal documents of the Bank that the technical personnel, notably W. R. Burgess and Carl Snyder, were the most consistent supporters of expansionary measures on a large scale. Perhaps because of these doubts, perhaps because of his overriding desire to secure consensus, Harrison continued to present to the rest of the System purchase proposals scaled down well below the level that some of the directors and technical personnel of the Bank regarded as desirable.

[92] Miscellaneous, Vol. I, letter, dated July 3, 1930, Harrison to all governors.

within the System until the 1950's, the emphasis was exclusively on credit conditions rather than the stock of money. However, the omission did not affect the policy conclusion; it only altered the line of argument through which it was reached. Consideration of the behavior of the stock of money would have led to precisely the same conclusion: that the System should act so as to prevent a reduction in the amount of high-powered money available and indeed so as to increase it. Moreover, as we saw in section 3, there was a particularly close connection at the time between the bond market and the money stock. Improvement in the bond market would have done much to avert the subsequent bank failures. And though this connection was not explicit in the letter, it was implicit.[93] Harrison's letter and the replies to it provide an extraordinarily illuminating and comprehensive picture of attitudes toward monetary matters within the System. Only two governors—Eugene Black of Atlanta and George Seay of Richmond—clearly and unambiguously agreed with Harrison's analysis and supported his policy recommendations. The rest disagreed, most of them sharply.

James McDougal of Chicago wrote that it seemed to him there was "an abundance of funds in the market, and under these circumstances, as a matter of prudence . . . it should be the policy of the Federal Reserve System to maintain a position of strength, in readiness to meet future demands, as and when they arise, rather than to put reserve funds into the market when not needed." He went on to stress the danger that "speculation might easily arise in some other direction" than in the stock market. McDougal had all along been the most outspoken opponent of the New York policy and was to remain for the rest of the contraction a consistent proponent of selling government securities on almost any occasion. The demands for which the System should husband its resources remained in the future. McDougal's outlook was particularly influential because Chicago was next only to New York in importance as a financial center, and because he had been with the System so long. McDougal had been appointed governor of the Chicago Bank at its founding in 1914, at the same time Strong was appointed governor in New York. He had had disagreements with New York on earlier occasions.[94]

[93] One important advantage of explicit attention to the stock of money, both on that occasion and later, would have been provision of a clearly defined indicator by which to judge in quantitative terms the needs and effects of policy. The outsider is struck, in reading the reports of discussions within the System, by the vagueness and imprecision of the criteria used. For example, with the "needs of business" undefined, one participant regarded "credit," also undefined, as "redundant," another as "tight." Lack of a common universe of discourse and inability to reduce differences of opinion to quantitative terms were probably important factors enabling differences to persist for so long with no approach to a meeting of minds.

[94] Harrison, Miscellaneous, Vol. I, letter, dated July 10, 1930, McDougal to Harrison; Lester V. Chandler, *Benjamin Strong, Central Banker*, Brookings, 1958, pp. 79, 445.

John U. Calkins of San Francisco was no less explicit than McDougal was. In an earlier letter to Governor Young explaining why San Francisco had not participated in the June open market purchases, he had stated that "with credit cheap and redundant we do not believe that business recovery will be accelerated by making credit cheaper and more redundant." In his reply to Harrison's letter, he repeated the sentiment, expressed the view that "the creation, promotion, or encouragement of a bond market" is not "within the province of the Federal Reserve System," and that "no encouragement of the market for foreign bonds can counterbalance the destructive effect upon our foreign trade of the tariff bill recently approved." He went on to say, "We believe that the volume of credit forcibly fed to the market up to this time has had no considerable good effect, certainly no discernible effect in the last few months. We also believe that every time we inject further credit without appreciable effort, we diminish the probable advantage of feeding more to the market at an opportune moment which may come."[95]

Lynn P. Talley of Dallas wrote that his directors were not "inclined to countenance much interference with economic trends through artificial methods to compose situations that in themselves grow out of events recognized at the time as being fallacious"—a reference to the stock market speculation of 1928–29. Talley's letter, like some others, reveals resentment at New York's failure to carry the day in 1929 and the feeling that existing difficulties were the proper punishment for the System's past misdeeds in not checking the bull market. "If a physician," wrote Talley, "either neglects a patient, or even though he does all he can for the patient within the limits of his professional skill according to his best judgment, and the patient dies, it is conceded to be quite impossible to bring the patient back to life through the use of artificial respiration or injections of adrenalin."[96]

W. B. Geery of Minneapolis wrote that "there is danger of stimulating financing which will lead to still more overproduction while attempting to make it easy to do financing which will increase consumption."[97]

George W. Norris of Philadelphia replied that discussions with an insurance company executive and with a private banker in Philadelphia had confirmed him in his own view "of the fruitlessness and unwisdom of attempting to depress still further the abnormally low interest rates now prevailing." Later in the year, at a meeting of the Open Market Policy Conference in September, Norris, in strong disagreement with what he regarded as the current policy of the System, read a lengthy memorandum summarizing the Philadelphia view. The Philadelphia Bank objected to

[95] Miscellaneous, Vol. I, letter, dated June 16, 1930, Calkins to Young; letter, dated July 10, 1930, Calkins to Harrison.

[96] Miscellaneous, Vol. I, letter, dated July 15, 1930, Talley to Harrison.

[97] *Ibid.*, letter, dated July 7, 1930, Geery to Harrison.

"the present abnormally low rates for money" as an interference "with the operation of the natural law of supply and demand in the money market . . ." and concluded, "this is a complete and literal reversal of the policy stated in the Board's Tenth Annual Report . . . We have been putting out credit in a period of depression, when it was not wanted and could not be used, and will have to withdraw credit when it is wanted and can be used."[98]

These views, which seem to us confused and misguided, were by no means restricted to the Reserve System. The Federal Advisory Council, whose members were leading bankers throughout the country, consistently adopted recommendations expressing the same point of view, using phrases such as, "the present situation will be best served if the natural flow of credit is unhampered by open-market operations."[99] However, even in the financial community, the New York Reserve Bank was not alone in its view of the situation. The July 1930 monthly letter of the Royal

[98] Harrison, Miscellaneous, Vol. I, letter, dated July 8, Norris to Harrison; Open Market, Vol. I, memorandum read by Norris at Sept. 25, 1930, meeting. The memorandum is such a remarkably clear statement of the real bills doctrine that was so widely accepted at the time and earlier that it is worth quoting at greater length. The policy which had

> created artificially low interest rates, and artificially high prices for government securities . . . is an injustice to our member banks. It had resulted in making open market operations usurp the discount function, and tends to foster the regrettable impression that there is some element of impropriety in borrowing by member banks . . . [A]s the result of injecting a large amount of unasked and unneeded Federal Reserve credit into an already glutted money market, we find ourselves with over 600 millions of governments on hand, the bulk of which must ultimately be disposed of . . . We do not undertake to say how much Federal Reserve credit should be in use today, but we do hold to the belief that a substantial part of it should be the result of a demand expressed in borrowing by member banks, and used in cooperation with those banks. Less than one-sixth of it is of this character today.

In addition to the letters quoted, and the two from Black and Seay, a brief letter was sent to Harrison by O. M. Attebery, deputy governor at St. Louis, on behalf of Governor Martin, on vacation, expressing doubts and stating that conditions in the Eighth District provided no justification for further open market purchases (Miscellaneous, Vol. I, letter, dated July 9, 1930). Frederic H. Curtiss, chairman of the Boston Bank, sent a lengthy letter dated July 9 (the Boston Bank at the time had no governor, Harding having died in April, and Young, still governor of the Board, not yet having been appointed to fill the Boston Bank vacancy). Curtiss' letter expressed strong opposition to further purchases on the ground that they were likely to feed the stock market rather than the bond market. Only the Federal Reserve Bank of Cleveland did not reply, but its governor acknowledged the letter by telephone. In a letter to Governor Young, Harrison summarized the views expressed by Governor Fancher of Cleveland on his own behalf and as spokesman for a majority of his directors, "that continued purchases of government securities would not contribute substantially to . . . recovery and that, therefore, they would not . . . favor further purchases" (Miscellaneous, Vol. I, letter, dated July 23, 1930, Harrison to Young).

[99] Quoted from recommendation, dated Nov. 18, 1930 (Federal Reserve Board, *Annual Report* for 1930, p. 228).

Bank of Canada concluded that "immediate and decisive action on the part of the Federal Reserve Banks in putting new funds into the market in large volume is what is necessary to arrest the present serious and protracted price decline and to change the present psychology of business."

One cannot read the correspondence with Harrison just reviewed, the minutes of open market meetings, and similar Reserve System documents without being impressed with the extraordinary differences between New York and most of the other Banks in the level of sophistication and understanding about monetary matters. Years of primary and direct responsibility for the conduct of monetary policy in the central money market of the country and of cooperation with men similarly placed in the other leading money markets of the world had developed in the technical personnel, officers, and directors of the New York Bank a profound awareness of monetary relations and a sensitive recognition of the effects of monetary policy actions. Those qualities were clearly absent at most other Reserve Banks, which had of necessity been concerned primarily with local and regional matters, or at the Federal Reserve Board, which had played only a minor role in the general conduct of policy and had had no important operating functions.

The largely negative response evoked by Harrison's letter induced New York on several occasions during July to consider again engaging in open market purchases on its own but with the approval of the Board, and Harrison sounded out the sentiment of the Board about such action. The results were sufficiently unfavorable to deter any attempt.[100]

By September, 1930, some of the Banks were even opposed to seasonal easing. As Harrison told his directors,

Some of the other Federal Reserve Banks, including perhaps a majority of the banks whose governors form the executive committee of the System Open Market Policy Conference, advocate a policy of correction rather than of anticipation. They would allow tightening of the money market and hardening of rates of interest to develop, and then would move to correct the situation through the purchase of Government securities.

A few days later, when Carl Snyder, at a meeting of the officers' council of the New York Bank, suggested that "this deflation should now be aggressively combatted by additional purchases of Government securities . . . ," Harrison replied that "from a System standpoint it is a practical impossibility to embark on such a program at the present time—to do so would mean an active division of System policy."[101]

Despite the decline in Federal Reserve credit outstanding, the Board described its policy for the year 1930 as one of "monetary ease . . . expressed through the purchase at intervals of additional United States

[100] Harrison, Notes, Vol. I, July 10, 24, 1930; and Office, Vol. II, June 5, 1930.
[101] Notes, Vol. I, Sept. 11, 17, 1930.

Government securities and in progressive reductions of reserve bank discount and acceptance rates."[102] This is a striking illustration of the ambiguity of the terms "monetary ease" and "tightness" and of the need stressed above (p. 272) to interpret Federal Reserve actions in the light of all the forces affecting the stock of money and credit conditions. It seems paradoxical to describe as "monetary ease" a policy which permitted the stock of money to decline in fourteen months by a percentage exceeded only four times in the preceding fifty-four years and then only during extremely severe business-cycle contractions. And those words seem especially paradoxical when other factors were tending to expand the money stock, so that a potential expansion was converted into an actual contraction entirely by the decline in Federal Reserve credit outstanding.

In the context of the changes then occurring in the economy and in the money markets, the policy followed should be regarded as one of monetary "tightness" not "ease." During a period of severe economic contraction extending over more than a year, the System was content to let its discounts decline by nearly twice its net purchases of government securities, and to let its total credit outstanding decline by almost three times the increase in the gold stock. Through early 1932, the most striking feature of the System's portfolio of government securities and bills bought is the usual seasonal pattern of contraction during the first half of the year and expansion during the second. From August 1929 to October 1930, the whole increase in government securities plus bills bought came in the second half of 1929. The System's holdings of government securities plus bills bought were nearly $200 million lower at the end of July 1930 than they were at the end of December 1929. Even a mechanical continuation of the System's earlier gold sterilization program, by which it had quite explicitly recognized the need to determine its actions in light of other factors outside its control, would have called for more vigorous expansionary action from August 1929 to October 1930. Such action would have limited the decline in Federal Reserve credit outstanding to $210 million, the magnitude of the rise in the gold stock, instead of allowing the actual seasonally adjusted decline of $590 million. As we read the earlier policy statements of the Board, they called for going beyond mechanical gold sterilization in view of contemporary economic conditions. Since the bull market in stocks had collapsed and there were no signs of anything approaching speculation in commodities, any expansion in credit would be likely to be, in the words of the *Tenth Annual Report* (for 1923), "restricted to productive uses."[103]

---

[102] Federal Reserve Board, *Annual Report* for 1930, p. 1.

[103] It should be noted, however, that the possibility that easy money conditions might stimulate speculative excesses in the stock market was a recurrent theme in

The stalemate within the System continued, with only minor variations, throughout the next year. Harrison was pressed on the one side by his officers and directors—though less consistently by the directors than in the preceding year—to work for greater easing and larger purchases. On the other side, he felt strongly his responsibilities, as chairman of the Open Market Policy Conference, to carry out loyally the policy adopted by the Conference. The one major difference in the situation was the replacement of Roy Young by Eugene Meyer as governor of the Federal Reserve Board. Young became governor of the Boston Bank in September 1930 and, as such, was a member of the executive committee of the Conference, where he joined McDougal in consistently opposing purchases and favoring sales.[104] Meyer was generally favorable toward purchases and, not having gone through Harrison's frustrating experience of 1930, inclined to press strongly for them.

The January 1931 meeting of the Open Market Policy Conference brought out clearly the changes in the situation. From October to mid-December 1930, there had been virtually no change in the System's holdings of government securities. The banking difficulties in New York following the failure of the Bank of United States in the second week of December necessitated purchase of $45 million of government securities by the New York Reserve Bank for its own account. They were bought from two banks undergoing heavy withdrawals of currency in order to enable them to avoid borrowing. In addition, $80 million of government securities were purchased for System account, as Harrison explained, "in order to avoid too great tightening of credit due to an unusual amount of 'window dressing'." The purchases were made in accordance with the authorization by the Conference meeting on September 25, 1930, as a compromise between the advocates of "anticipation" and "correction," of purchases up to $100 million for seasonal ease.[105] At its January 1931

---

the deliberations of the period, e.g., Harrison, Miscellaneous, Vol. I, letter, dated Mar. 17, 1930, J. H. Case (chairman of the New York Bank) to Governor Young; Notes, Vol. I, Apr. 24, 1930; Miscellaneous, Vol. I, letter, dated Apr. 29, Harrison to Platt; *ibid.,* letter, dated July 10, 1930, J. B. McDougal to Harrison.

[104] According to Hamlin, Young was eased out of his position on the Board because of the administration's disappointment with his leadership. If so, the result could hardly have been the one intended. As governor of the Boston Bank and a member of the executive committee of the Conference, he may well have been in a position to exercise a stronger influence on open market operations, the key area in which policy had been and continued to be unsatisfactory, than he could have exercised as governor of the Federal Reserve Board (see Hamlin, Diary, Vol. 18, Sept. 4, 6, 24; Oct. 3, 10; Nov. 24, 1930, pp. 67, 70, 84, 89, 91–93, 118–119).

[105] See Harrison, Open Market, Vol. I, minutes of meeting, Jan. 21, 1931, in which Harrison reviewed changes in the money market since the Sept. 25, 1930, meeting. See also a memorandum, prepared for Harrison by W. R. Burgess, dated Dec. 19, 1930, referring to the absence of change in the System account between Sept. 25, 1930, and the date of the memorandum. The purchases by New York up

meeting, the Open Market Policy Conference recommended that "it would be desirable to dispose of some of the System holdings of government securities as and when opportunity affords itself to do this without disturbance or any tightening of the money position."[106] When the members of the Reserve Board met subsequently with the governors, both Adolph Miller and Eugene Meyer objected. Harrison, in his capacity as chairman of the Conference, defended the recommendation on the ground that it "represented a compromise since some of those present were in favor of considerable sales of securities, while others were only in favor of such moderate sales as might be necessary to take up the slack." Meyer, sensitive to political repercussions, stated that

a reduction of bills and discounts of the System did not involve the launching of any major policy, whereas the sale of governments is commonly interpreted as a major move in Federal reserve policy. The Reserve System has been accused in a number of quarters of pursuing a deflationary policy in the past year, and a sale of government securities at this time is likely to draw fire. In this situation it would appear most desirable to avoid a move which appears to present a major change in policy when there is no necessity for doing it.

Despite Meyer's reservations, the Board approved the Conference's recommendation and, by February 1931, security holdings had fallen by $130 million, although there was concern about the associated tightening of the bond market.[107]

---

to that date were only $40 million from one large bank. The purchases for System account after Dec. 20 were made by New York at its own discretion, the executive committee at a meeting on that day in Washington with Governor Meyer and several Board members having agreed "to leave it to the judgment of the Federal Reserve Bank of New York whether some additional amount of government securities should be purchased within the $100,000,000 authority with the understanding that the New York bank would keep in close communication with the members of the committee" (*ibid.*, minutes of executive committee meeting, Dec. 20, 1930).

[106] The original resolution as passed had the word "undue" (later deleted) before "tightening."

[107] Harrison, Open Market, Vol. II, minutes of meeting, Jan. 21, 1931, and letter, dated Jan. 29, 1931, McClelland (for Board) to Harrison, approving the recommendation; Notes, Vol. I, Jan. 15, 19, 22, 1931.

A memorandum on the Open Market Policy Conference meeting of Jan. 21, 1931, written by E. A. Goldenweiser, the Federal Reserve System's director of research, stated:

Meyer strongly opposes sales of securities beyond the amount bought in December for seasonal and special purposes . . . . The rest of the governors did not change their minds, but were impressed by Meyer's sincerity and force. It appears to have been his first bout with the intrenched hard-money crowd of the Federal reserve system.

The memorandum is part of the Goldenweiser Papers in the Manuscript Division of the Library of Congress (Container 1, folder of Confidential Memoranda,

In April 1931, Harrison, as chairman of the Open Market Policy Conference, presented a report to the Governors Conference. He expressed great concern about the gold inflow and the dangers to the world of continued gold sterilization by the United States.[108] As to the domestic situation, he noted:

> While it is commonly stated that money conditions have been exceedingly easy in recent months, and while indeed money rates have been at very low levels there has not been over a period of months any consistent surplus of Federal reserve funds pressing for use upon the market . . . . Furthermore, apart from the relatively easy position of the banks in the larger cities, credit cannot be said to be very cheap or very plentiful generally throughout the country.[109]

Harrison's report was discussed at the Open Market Policy Conference, which approved, at his urging, a three-part program to make gold imports more effective and credit more active: maintenance of the bill portfolio, if possible; reduction of buying rates on bills and, less definitely, of discount rates; and—as a last resort, if bills purchased did not enable earning assets to be maintained—authority for the executive committee to purchase up to $100 million of government securities. The resolution including the final part of this mild program—the only part within the Conference's exclusive jurisdiction—was adopted with four reluctant supporters, three of the four, members of the executive committee.[110]

No purchases were made under that recommendation until after a June 22 meeting of the executive committee, at which Harrison urged purchases of $50 million. Meyer, who was present at the meeting, strongly supported Harrison, saying that "the Federal Reserve Board would . . . have some preference for a larger program of purchases . . . ." The authorization was granted with only one negative vote (Young of Boston), because Norris of Philadelphia abstained and McDougal of Chicago voted against his convictions out of deference to President Hoover's proposal, announced two days earlier, of a moratorium on intergovernmental debts ("purchases of governments would be received by the public as supporting the President's announcement"). On July 9, the executive

---

1922–33). Of the seven cardboard letter files (described as containers in the Division's records), only six are open to readers; the seventh may be opened before 1965 only upon written permission from Mrs. Goldenweiser. Only a small fraction of the open collection contains current analyses of Federal Reserve policy in 1919–45, the period of Goldenweiser's service with the Board. The Goldenweiser Papers are meager in coverage compared to the Harrison Papers and provide a far less comprehensive view from within the Federal Reserve System than the Hamlin Diary does. Consequently, we have made only minor use of them.

[108] See quotation from his report in sect. 4, above.

[109] Open Market, Vol. II, Apr. 27, 1931.

[110] Norris of Philadelphia, Young of Boston, and McDougal of Chicago. The fourth was Calkins of San Francisco (*ibid.*, minutes of meeting, Apr. 29, 1931).

committee agreed to a further purchase of $50 million to complete the $100 million authorized in April, but buying was stopped on July 16 at only $30 million because of Harrison's concern over foreign developments and despite the remonstrances of Meyer.[111]

By early August, Harrison and Meyer again pressed for purchases. In discussing the situation with the executive committee of directors of the New York Bank, Meyer presented figures showing that between November 1, 1930, and August 5, 1931, there had been "a total increase of $421,000,000 in the gold stock of the United States; that currency circulation had increased $350,000,000 instead of showing a normal seasonal decline of at least $100,000,000; and that the Bank of France had withdrawn about $125,000,000 from the market" (presumably the acceptance market). He then pointed out that "while there had been no intentional contraction of the base on which credit could be extended, the sterilization of an amount larger than the gain of gold had been passively permitted." He said that, "if we had been asked last November whether we would favor, or even permit, the sterilization of $400,000,000 of gold, undoubtedly we would have answered in the negative."[112]

When a majority of the executive committee of the Open Market Policy Conference proved to be unwilling to support further purchases, a meeting of the full Conference was called for August 11. Harrison proposed a program, to be put into effect when desirable, authorizing the executive committee to buy up to $300 million of government securities. Other governors, except Black of Atlanta who joined Harrison in favor of it, were entirely negative in their reaction, and the Conference voted instead an authorization for the executive committee to buy or sell $120 million.[113]

So far as we can discover, that was the first Conference meeting at which there was explicit reference to a problem later to be cited as a major reason for the Reserve System's failure to make any extensive security purchases—the problem of free gold. However, the free gold problem, to be discussed in the next section, played no role in the outcome.

When the Conference met the same day with members of the Board, Harrison was again in the position of having to present and defend a recommendation he did not favor. He explained that the Conference opposed immediate purchases of large amounts of government securities, because banks would not employ excess reserves. The banks' reason:

[111] Harrison, Open Market, Vol. II, minutes of executive meeting, June 22, 1931; Miscellaneous, Vol. I, letter, dated July 9, 1931, Harrison to Seay; Notes, Vol. I, July 16, 23, 1931.

[112] Notes, Vol. II, Aug. 10, 1931.

[113] Open Market, Vol. II, minutes of executive committee meeting, Aug. 4, 1931; minutes of meeting, Aug. 11, 1931. The $120 million included the usual $100 million plus the $20 million authorized in April but not used.

"most prime investments are selling on a very low yield basis, while secondary bonds consist largely of railroad issues, of which a considerable proportion may in a short time become ineligible for investment by savings banks, insurance companies, and trust funds, due to the provisions of various state laws. In addition the bond market has been uncertain because of pressure on the market, due to forced liquidation of bond portfolios of closed banks." Governor Meyer and other members of the Board expressed disappointment at the action taken by the Conference, "in that it limited possible purchases to an ineffective amount." However, the only consequence of their disappointment was a change in the timing of the Board's session with the Conference. Thereafter, the two bodies discussed policy actions before rather than after the Conference adopted its recommendation. Later, when the Board formally considered the recommendation, it did not approve it outright but delegated to Governor Meyer the authority to approve purchases but not sales.[114] In the event, not even the $120 million authorization was carried out.

BRITAIN'S DEPARTURE FROM GOLD, SEPTEMBER 1931

Britain's departure from gold and the resulting gold outflow from the United States changed the focus of policy-making from the Open Market Policy Conference back to the New York Bank. New York had always had, and continued to have, primary responsibility for international monetary relations. The Bank of England, the Bank of France, and other central banks had always treated the New York Bank as their counterpart and had conducted negotiations and consultations with it. The Board had been kept informed, consulted in the process, and its approval obtained

[114] Harrison, Open Market, Vol. II, minutes of meetings, Aug. 11, Nov. 30, 1931; and letter, dated Aug. 18, 1931, Meyer to Harrison.

Though Harrison was in agreement with Meyer on the substance of the policy issue, he was disturbed by the Board's response to the Conference recommendation, and complained to Meyer that it was contrary to the rules adopted when the Conference was established. To his own board of directors, Harrison stated:

. . . the whole situation emphasized the inherent difficulties of existing open market procedure. Direction of system policies by a conference of twelve men who must also consult the Federal Reserve Board means . . . that . . . we run a real risk of having no policy at all. Some of the Federal reserve bank governors . . . attended the Conference with preconceived ideas which would not admit of argument, and others in spite of, or perhaps because of, the fact that their banks would not be able to participate in further purchases of government securities, looked at the whole question from the narrow standpoint of their individual position (Notes, Vol. II, Aug. 20, 1931).

Commenting on the results of that meeting of the Conference, Governor Meyer said, according to Hamlin, that "Governor Harrison could present a matter very gracefully, but could not sell it; that if the Board had taken part in the conference, he believed the Governors would have followed the Board and the New York bank" (Hamlin, Diary, Vol. 19, Aug. 11, 1931, p. 129). He may have been right on this occasion, but later experience suggests that he was unduly sanguine.

before final action, but it had never had a major voice in forming policy. The other Reserve Banks had for the most part simply been kept informed. That had been the practice while Strong was alive and had remained the practice. The most recent instance during the contraction had been the negotiations in the summer of 1931 in connection with loans to foreign banks.

New York had little doubt about what action to take. At its October 8 meeting, the board of directors voted to raise the discount rate from $1\frac{1}{2}$ to $2\frac{1}{2}$ per cent. The arguments given at the meeting were, first, the gold outflow itself, and second, "advices from France, where foreign fears concerning the dollar appear to have concentrated, which indicated that an increase in the rate would be interpreted there more favorably than otherwise." Some fear was expressed that the rise in rates might have adverse domestic effects, particularly by interfering with Hoover's efforts to organize a National Credit Corporation, but that fear was belittled. Harrison noted that any unfavorable effect on the bond market could be offset by security purchases, since the executive committee of the Open Market Policy Conference still had authority, under the recommendation of the August 11 meeting, to buy up to $120 million of government securities.[115] The only discordant note was a cablegram from Burgess, who was in Europe on a mission for the Bank, recommending no action that would bring about higher money rates in the United States.[116] The cablegram was read at the meeting, then disregarded. The Reserve Board promptly approved the rise in discount rates, several of its members having been strongly in favor of a rise ever since the beginning of the gold drain.[117]

A week later, Eugene Meyer attended the directors' meeting at the New York Bank. Harrison proposed a further increase in the discount rate to $3\frac{1}{2}$ per cent, giving as the technical reason the continued gold outflow. One director, Charles E. Mitchell, expressed serious doubts about the domestic effects. Meyer replied that "an advance in the rate was called

[115] However, three days earlier, at a meeting of the executive committee of the board of directors, Harrison said that "he considered the gold position of the System paramount at this time and on that account would not be inclined to purchase Government securities" (Harrison, Notes, Vol. II, Oct. 5, 1931).

[116] Burgess had arrived in Europe on Oct. 9 to attend a regular monthly meeting at Basle of the Bank for International Settlements. It was the first time a Federal Reserve official had formally participated in discussions of European central bankers at the world bank. The New York Bank was not a member, because it had been forbidden by the State Department to subscribe to shares of the BIS when the latter was formed in 1930. However, there were unofficial ties between the two institutions, strengthened by the fact that Gates W. McGarrah, president of the BIS, had formerly been chairman of the New York Bank.

[117] Hamlin and Miller, at least, strongly favored an increase in discount rates and considered a possible effect on the bond market as no valid reason for delay (Hamlin, Diary, Vol. 19, Oct. 1, 1931, p. 148).

for by every known rule, and that . . . foreigners would regard it as a lack of courage if the rate were not advanced." He expressed the opinion that "the bond market was already adjusted to a higher level of interest rates, and therefore it would be but little affected."[118] A month later, Owen D. Young pressed the desirability of purchasing government securities to offset unfavorable domestic effects. Harrison was exceedingly hesitant to accede.[119]

The sharp rises in discount rates were widely supported not only within the System but also outside.[120] The maintenance of the gold standard was accepted as an objective in support of which men of a broad range of views were ready to rally. The drain of gold was a dramatic event for which there were many precedents.[121] Thus both the problem and its solution seemed clear and straightforward. Indeed, one gets the impression that after grappling with unfamiliar, elusive, and subtle problems, the System greeted with almost a sense of relief the emergence of a problem that could be put in black-and-white terms.

Less than two weeks after the second rise in discount rates, the executive committee of the Open Market Policy Conference met. The preliminary memorandum for the meeting outlined the drastic change that had occurred in currency in circulation, pointed out that internal developments had been more important than the gold outflows in their effects on domestic business, and noted that the decline in deposits "constitutes by far the most rapid shrinkage in member bank deposits during the life of the System." Nevertheless, McDougal continued to recommend that the System should reduce its security holdings, although—in addition to the unprecedented pressure on commercial banks at the time—it was the beginning of the season when the System typically expanded its security holdings. The final outcome was a vote against sales but in favor of requesting the Federal Reserve Board to give the committee the same leeway for sales that the Board had given it for purchases under the Conference recommendation of August 11.[122]

---

[118] Harrison, Notes, Vol. II, Oct. 15, 1931.

[119] *Ibid.*, Nov. 25, 1931.

[120] "We think the really constructive event of the week has been . . . the action of the New York Federal Reserve Bank in raising its rediscount rate . . . . This step should have been taken long ago, and, indeed, it was a sad error of judgment to put such a fantastically low rate as that at New York in force. . ." (*Commercial and Financial Chronicle*, Oct. 10, 1931, p. 2305). ". . . [T]he Federal Reserve Bank of New York has been driven into making another advance of a full 1% in its rediscount rate . . . , a decidedly wise move. . . " (*ibid.*, Oct. 17, 1931, p. 3460). The New York *Times* reported that the rise was "welcomed by almost all bankers" (Oct. 11, 1931); that the rise was "hailed with enthusiasm in banking circles" (Oct. 16, 1931).

[121] See, however, further discussion in sect. 6, below.

[122] Harrison, Open Market, Vol. II, memorandum and minutes of executive committee meeting, Oct. 26, 1931. In the course of the meeting, Harrison noted that "the free gold position . . . was not a consideration at this time. . . ."

The preliminary memorandum for a meeting of the full Conference at the end of November noted with satisfaction that the "foreign and domestic drains upon bank reserves were met in the classic way by increases in discount rates combined with a policy of free lending." It recorded that "one result" of the rise in discount rates and the associated rise in other market rates "was certainly to make bankers and others more timid and reluctant in contemplating new uses of funds or new enterprises." It stressed the sharp decline in bond prices and the resulting worsening of the position of the banks. It discussed the year-end seasonal problem, suggesting that purchases "similar to those made last year" should be provided for, and proposed deferring the longer-term policy decisions until after the first of the year. The Conference adopted a resolution giving the executive committee authority to purchase up to $200 million of governments for seasonal needs.[123] Only part of that authority was in fact exercised. Government security holdings were raised by $75 million to the end of December 1931 and then lowered by $50 million in January 1932.

During those months, it is not clear that Harrison was as unhappy with the policy followed as he had been before and was to be again. His concern about gold inhibited his desire to expand Federal Reserve credit. New York still had control over the buying rate on bills, subject only to the approval of the Board. As we have seen, New York had repeatedly tried to use bill purchases to enable it to accomplish on its own what it could not accomplish through the System open market account. Yet the bill buying rate, which had been raised from $1\frac{1}{4}$ per cent to $3\frac{1}{8}$ per cent in October along with the discount rate, was reduced only slowly and moderately, to 3 per cent on November 20, and to $2\frac{3}{4}$ per cent on January 12, 1932. Both reductions left the rate above the market rate and therefore did not lead to an increase in bill holdings.

Early in January 1932, partly under pressure from his staff and directors, Harrison resumed his advocacy of a program of further substantial purchases as part of a broader national program which he outlined to the meeting of the Open Market Policy Conference that month. The main features of the program were: passage of an act establishing the Reconstruction Finance Corporation, then under consideration by Congress; organized support of the bond market, predicated on an agreement between the railroads and the unions to cut wage rates; cooperation of Federal Reserve Banks and member banks with the Treasury in its financing program; purchase of bills by the Reserve System when possible; reductions in discount rates; and, as a final step, "buying of Governments, if necessary, facilitated by an alleviation of the free gold position," the

[123] Governor McDougal asked assurance at the meeting that no purchases would be made immediately. Governors Norris and Fancher said "they were not disposed to approve of the purchase of government securities solely for the purpose of enabling the New York and Chicago banks to keep out of debt at the end of the year" (*ibid.*, memorandum and minutes of meeting, Nov. 30, 1931).

final phrase being a reference to proposals then under consideration which were finally embodied in the Glass-Steagall Act. The Conference authorized the executive committee to purchase up to $200 million, "if necessary," over three negative votes.[124] That authorization was not exercised at all. Between the January 11 and February 24, 1932, meetings of the Conference, government security holdings declined by $11 million, bill holdings by $80 million, while discounts rose $20 million. Federal Reserve credit outstanding fell by $100 million over the six-week period.

The February meeting of the Open Market Policy Conference was largely a repetition of the January meeting, although the pending passage of the Glass-Steagall Act removed the problem of free gold. At the joint meeting with the Board preceding the formal business session, Meyer, who continued as governor of the Board though he had by then been named chairman of the RFC as well, asserted that "it seemed unnecessary for the banking position to be subjected to severe strain because of the funds withdrawn for hoarding." Miller stated that "he believed there was never a safer time to operate boldly than at present." He indicated that "he would approve purchases on an even larger scale than the amounts being discussed." McDougal continued to argue that "on general principles he preferred to see the banks borrowing to secure funds." The upshot was a mild expansion in the authority of the executive committee. It was authorized to buy up to $250 million at the approximate rate of $25 million a week, McDougal and Young voting in the negative. Immediately after the general meeting, the executive committee voted 3 to 2 to start the program.[125]

OPEN MARKET PURCHASE PROGRAM OF 1932

That modest program would very likely never have been expanded into a major one, or perhaps even carried out, if it had not been for direct and indirect pressure from Congress. Harrison told the executive committee of his directors on April 4 that apparently "the only way to forestall some sort of radical financial legislation by Congress, is to go further and faster with our own program." When Harrison reported to a full meeting of his directors on April 7 that the executive committee of the Open Market Policy Conference was deeply divided about the wisdom of accelerating the purchase program, and had voted to continue the existing program, one of the directors asked "if a more vigorous program

[124] Harrison, Open Market, Vol. II, minutes of meeting, Jan. 11, 1932. McDougal of Chicago, Seay of Richmond, and Deputy Governor Day, representing Governor Calkins of San Francisco, were the three who voted in the negative. Neither Governor Young nor any other representative of the Boston Bank attended the meeting. The Kansas City Bank was represented by a director who was not present at the session when the resolution was adopted.

[125] *Ibid.*, minutes of meeting, Feb. 24, 1932.

on the part of the Federal Reserve System would not be helpful in defeating the Thomas bonus bill and other similar legislation. Governor Harrison said that Senator Thomas had indicated to him that he might be satisfied not to press for Congressional action if the System would proceed more vigorously." The Bank directors accordingly voted to have the Bank, subject to the approval of the Board, buy for its own account up to $50 million of government securities, outside the System account and before the meeting of the Conference, which was set for April 12.[126]

In opening the joint meeting of the Conference and the Reserve Board, preceding the business meeting of the Conference, Governor Meyer "called attention, merely as a matter of information, to the fact that a resolution had been offered in the Senate asking the Federal Reserve Board to state its program . . . . Consideration of this resolution had been postponed. He stated that the Reserve System could now undertake to do more toward aiding in the recovery than it had yet done, and that he believed the time had come when the System might be expected to use its powers more fully in an effort to stop the credit decline." Other members of the Board supported Meyer. Ogden L. Mills, since February 13, 1932, Secretary of the Treasury, who had all along been in favor of more extensive action, stated: "For a great central banking system to stand by with a 70% gold reserve without taking active steps in such a situation was almost inconceivable and almost unforgivable. The resources of the System should be put to work on a scale commensurate with the existing emergency."

After the Board left, the Conference voted 10 to 1 to approve a resolution offered by Harrison authorizing the executive committee to purchase up to $500 million of government securities in addition to the unexpired authority granted at the February 24 meeting. The purchases were to be made as rapidly as practicable and, if possible, to be no less than $100 million in the current statement week ending next day, April 13.[127] The

---

[126] Notes, Vol. II, Apr. 4, 7, 1932.

[127] The lone dissenter was Governor Young of the Boston Bank, who had said at the joint session with the Board that he

questioned whether purchases of governments which piled up reserves in the centers would result in the distribution of these funds to other parts of the country. He was skeptical of getting the cooperation of the banks without which success appeared difficult, and was apprehensive that a program of this sort would develop the animosity of many bankers, and was apprehensive also that an extensive program of purchases of government securities would impair the confidence of the public in the Reserve banks. He cited the experience of 1931 as an indication of the futility of government purchases.

Governor McDougal of Chicago asked whether the Reserve System "could retain the confidence of the public after inaugurating a policy of this sort, which was in some measure inflationary, particularly since it involved the use of government securities as collateral for Federal reserve notes" (Harrison, Open Market, Vol. II, minutes of meeting, Apr. 12, 1932).

final proviso was inserted after Harrison had informed the Conference he was scheduled to testify the next day before a subcommittee of the House on a bill that in effect would have directed the Reserve System to purchase in the open market until wholesale prices had risen to their 1926 level. He said that "it would probably be necessary for him to make some reference to the program at that time."[128]

After the initial program was voted on April 12, the System bought $100 million of government securities per week for five weeks. At the May 17 meeting, the Conference again voted another $500 million open market purchase, McDougal joining Young in dissenting. At the suggestion of Meyer, the weekly rate of purchases after that meeting was reduced. Harrison deplored the reduction: "The temper of Congress is not improving, and the danger of unsound credit proposals is still great. It might, therefore, be unwise to give unnecessary substance to the argument now being used, that the Federal Reserve System intends soon to abandon its open market program." Yet in June, partly no doubt in the hope of conciliating McDougal and Young, he suggested to the executive committee of the Conference that the purchases each week be geared to the maintenance of member bank excess reserves at a figure somewhere between $250 and $300 million, the purchases to be as small as possible to preserve the desired level, but with some increase from week to week in the System's holdings, "to avoid the creation of a feeling that the policy of the system had been changed."[129]

By the end of June, as Burgess summarized the results of the program for the New York directors, total purchases of $1 billion had offset a loss of $500 million in gold and a reduction of $400 million in discounts and bills bought, leaving a net increase of $100 million in Federal Reserve credit outstanding. To Owen D. Young, this meant that "most of our efforts had, in reality, served to check a contraction of credit rather than to stimulate an expansion of credit. We have been clearing the way for action, rather than taking action. . . ." A week later, in discussing the pressure from Chicago and Boston to stop the program, he said,

As it is, we are asked to stop when we are just half way through our program, when we are just at the point where further purchases of Government securities

---

[128] The hearings, which threatened to develop into a full-scale investigation of the System, were held by the House Subcommittee on Banking and Currency on H.R. 10517 (a bill to stabilize commodity prices, introduced by Rep. T. Alan Goldsborough). Governor Harrison testified that the Federal Reserve "began to really utilize the" Glass-Steagall Act only two days before he appeared before the committee (*Congressional Record,* House, June 8, 1932, p. 12354, remarks of Mr. Goldsborough). See also *Stabilization of Commodity Prices,* Hearings before the House Subcommittee on Banking and Currency, 72d Cong., 1st sess., part 2, pp. 477–478, 500–501.

[134] Harrison, Open Market, Vol. II. Meyer was referring to the series of bills 1932; Notes, Vol. II, May 26, 1932.

will bring actual and affirmative pressure to bear upon the member banks . . . . To stop just when you have reached the place where you are able to put on the pressure the program was designed to produce, would be a ridiculous thing to do. We shall have no policy left if we do this.[130]

Chicago and Boston took those same facts as evidence in favor of their opposition to the program, as evidence that it had only substituted an undesirable form of credit for a desirable form. McDougal, reported Harrison, "does not see what the purchases have done anyway, and is in favor of stopping." Governor Young felt "that there are going to be a lot more banks closed, that there will be a large increase in borrowing at the Federal reserve banks and that, therefore, we are wasting our resources buying Government securities."[131]

Some officers of the New York Bank, notably Burgess, and some directors favored continuing the program, with the approval of the Board, even if that meant New York would have to proceed without Chicago and Boston. Since the Reserve Board was in favor of continuing the program, it doubtless would have approved. But Harrison was unwilling to follow that course. The gold reserve ratio of the New York Bank was only 50 per cent, of the System 58 per cent, of Chicago 75 per cent. Yet Chicago was reluctant to participate. His own feeling, Harrison said, "is that we should continue with our open market program, and perhaps step it up a bit, but on one condition—that the program be made a real System program and that the Federal Reserve Banks of Boston and Chicago, in particular, give it their affirmative support." When the comment was made that the Board had the legal power to require other Banks to rediscount for New York, if its ratio fell below 50 per cent, Harrison replied "that it would be most undesirable for us to go ahead in defiance of the wishes of the other Federal reserve banks and then to have those banks bale us out under compulsion. System policy and the system Open Market Policy Conference might just as well be thrown out the window under such circumstances."[132]

At that juncture, Harrison made a final effort to secure the cooperation of Boston and Chicago. He pleaded the case not only with the governors and directors of the two Banks but also with commercial bankers and businessmen in the two cities. Owen D. Young made a trip to Chicago to

[130] Notes, Vol. II, June 30, July 5, 1932.

[131] Office, Vol. III, July 5, 1932; Notes, Vol. II, June 30, 1932.

[132] Notes, Vol. II, June 30, July 5, 1932. Harrison was at first attracted by the proposal that the Reserve Board bring pressure on the other Banks to participate in the purchase program. The Board's authority to compel one Reserve Bank to rediscount paper for another Reserve Bank, it was suggested, would apply also to purchases of government securities, when the reserve position of several Banks was involved (*ibid.,* June 30, 1932). On reconsideration, he decided that the Board had no power to bring such pressure, and that, "furthermore, this bank would be the first to object to such action by the Board, in other circumstances" (*ibid.,* July 5, 1932; see also July 11, 1932).

attempt to persuade the directors of the Chicago Bank. But all to no avail.[133]

In an attempt to decide the issue, the full Open Market Policy Conference met on July 14. At the joint meeting with the Board, Governor Meyer suggested that "in determining future policy it was important to consider that the public effect of any discontinuance of the policy which had been pursued would be unfortunate, and also that in future policy every effort should be made to secure an effective united system policy." He pointed out that "there existed a trend in Congress toward giving the System more centralization, and that the open market program offered a test of the capacity of the System to function effectively in its present form."[134] The Conference voted that excess reserves should be maintained

[133] Notes, Vol. II, July 7, 14, 1932; Office, Vol. III, letter, dated July 8, 1932, Harrison to Owen D. Young.

[134] Harrison, Open Market, Vol. II. Meyer was referring to the series of bills introduced by Senator Glass (see footnote 29, above), the most recent on Mar. 17, 1932, predecessors of the Banking Act of 1933. The latest bill was the occasion for a bitter exchange of letters between Glass and Harrison. With the approval of the New York Bank's directors, Harrison wrote to Senator Peter Norbeck, chairman of the Senate Banking and Currency Committee, enclosing a letter he had sent Glass, Feb. 6, about an earlier draft of the bill, which read in part as follows:

Many provisions of this bill are designed further to limit the autonomy of the individual Federal reserve banks and to concentrate more and more power in the Federal Reserve Board . . . . [T]he provisions of your bill relating to the open market committee which is given jurisdiction over operations in bills as well as government securities are so cumbersome as to be inimical to the best interest of Federal reserve operation . . . . The bill requires approval not only of the Federal Reserve Board but of a committee of 12 representatives of the several Federal reserve banks . . . . Under the proposed bill no operations in securities or bankers bills, even the day to day transactions, can be effected, even in cases of emergency, without approval of the committee . . . .
To the extent that your bill further shifts power and authority from the Federal reserve banks to the Federal Reserve Board, to that extent, I believe it aims towards centralized operation and control through a politically constituted body in Washington.

On Apr. 9, Glass answered Harrison's letter to Norbeck, writing:

In my considered view it constitutes a challenge to statutory authority and an unyielding antagonism to any restraining influence whatsoever.
. . . you and your board have thus stated in unequivocal terms the misconception of the Federal Reserve banking act which so long has been reflected in the extraordinary policies pursued by the New York bank with respect to both domestic and foreign transactions.

The "extraordinary policies" referred to by Glass, who was an undeviating follower of the real bills doctrine, included the use of open market operations in government securities and the failure to restrict loans to real bills only. In his eyes, the failure was responsible for both the boom and the bust.

Harrison's reply of Apr. 18 concluded the exchange:

The officers and directors of this bank have been just as desirous to do their part in checking the use of bank credit for excessive speculation as you or anyone

at approximately $200 million by purchases limited in total to the amount previously authorized by the Conference but not executed—$207 million. For the guidance of the executive committee, the Conference recommended purchases not to exceed $15 million a week—except in unusual or unforeseen circumstances—but not less than $5 million a week for the next four weeks. McDougal, Young, and Seay of Richmond voted against even this resolution.[135]

Freed from Congressional pressure—Congress adjourned on July 16—the Conference lapsed into its earlier pattern.[136] The program adopted was a minimum face-saving program, and was carried out at nearly the minimum level consistent with the letter of the recommendation. McDougal and Young refused to participate in further purchases. Harrison was unwilling to proceed on his own. As a consequence, in the four weeks after the Conference met, total purchases amounted to $30 million ($15 million the first week, then $5 million a week). From August 10 until the close of the year, the System's holdings remained almost precisely constant.

THE BANKING PANIC OF 1933

The preliminary memorandum for the January 4, 1933, meeting of the Open Market Policy Conference said of the existing situation, "that a good start was made toward recovery, that this movement has been interrupted, and is now hesitant and uncertain." At the meeting, both Governor Meyer and Secretary of the Treasury Mills stressed that any slackening in Federal Reserve open market policy might provide an excuse for the adoption of inflationary measures by Congress. Governor Harrison listed the Congressional situation as one of three reasons for holding the System portfolio of government securities intact; the second was that a reduction "might operate as a check to the bond market thus retarding business recovery and further injuring bond portfolios of banks;" the third

---

else. From their practical experience in operating a bank in this money center, they feel that in the long run there is only one really effective method of bringing about this result, and that is the traditional method of the vigorous use of discount rate and open market operations . . . . The tragedy of the experience of 1928 and 1929 lay, in our opinion, in the failure of the Reserve System promptly and vigorously to use the instruments for credit control which decades of experience have proved to be powerful and effective (Miscellaneous, Vol. II).

[135] Open Market, Vol. II, minutes of meeting, July 14, 1932.

[136] To the executive committee of the New York Bank's board of directors Harrison reported on July 11, 1932, a discussion he had had with Meyer in which "Governor Meyer agreed as to desirability of going ahead with the System open market program saying that, if for no other reason, it is politically impossible for us to stop at this particular time. The program was begun at about the time the Goldsborough Bill was introduced in Congress and if it were terminated just as Congress adjourned we would be crucified next winter" (Notes, Vol. II, July 11, 1932).

was that larger excess reserves might lead to the elimination of interest on deposits in principal centers, thus distributing "the pressure for putting money to work more widely." Against those three reasons, Harrison listed three others in favor of some reduction of the portfolio: first, the "System open market policy had not been one to accumulate any definite amount of securities but rather to check deflation through the reduction of bank debt and the creation of substantial excess reserves, which had been accomplished;" second, any further substantial increase in excess reserves might not increase pressure on the banks to lend and invest but would serve only to minimize control when necessary; third, the open market purchases had enabled the Treasury to borrow cheaply and "so in some measure has encouraged the continuance of an unbalanced budget."

The sentiment of most governors was clearly in favor of reducing the portfolio, and the final motion reflected that sentiment. It gave the executive committee authority to reduce the System's holdings of Treasury bills, the reduction in January not to exceed $125 million and not to bring excess reserves below $500 million. The committee was authorized to purchase securities if necessary to prevent excess reserves from falling below the existing level, but not if such purchases would do more than make up for declines in holdings. Before any increase in security holdings above the existing level was made, a new meeting of the Conference was to be convened.[137]

The policy recommendation was followed, and security holdings reduced by $90 million in January, despite the concern of Burgess and Treasury officials about the weakness of the bond market, and despite renewed banking difficulties. By February 1, 1933, excess reserves had fallen below $500 million, and the purchases made were not enough to restore that level. From the last week in January to February 15, the System increased its security holdings by $45 million, and permitted total Reserve credit to rise by $70 million. Yet, in those three weeks alone, member bank reserve balances at Federal Reserve Banks declined by $280 million.

The state to which open market operations—the most potent monetary tool of the System—had fallen was graphically revealed when, as the banking difficulties mounted in February, Harrison ruled out a meeting of the Conference on grounds that it would be "difficult, if not impossible, to hold a meeting of the system Open Market Policy Conference at this time." Instead, New York turned to bills as an alternative. On February 16, New York requested, and the Board approved, a reduction in its minimum buying rates on bills to ½ of 1 per cent. It acquired $350 million in

[137] Harrison, Open Market, Vol. II, preliminary memorandum, dated Dec. 31, 1932, and minutes of meeting, Jan. 4–5, 1933.

bills the following two weeks, though at the end of the second the Bank raised the bill rate twice, to 1 per cent on February 27, and to 1½ per cent on March 1, in consonance with rises in the discount rate. It also acquired $25 million of government securities in the first of the two weeks and $2 million in the second, primarily to enable banks to liquidate by selling government securities instead of borrowing on them.[138]

In the final two months prior to the banking holiday, there was nothing that could be called a System policy. The System was demoralized. Each Bank was operating on its own. All participated in the general atmosphere of panic that was spreading in the financial community and the community at large. The leadership which an independent central banking system was supposed to give the market and the ability to withstand the pressures of politics and of profit alike and to act counter to the market as a whole, these—the justification for establishing a quasi-governmental institution with broad powers—were conspicuous by their absence.

6. *Alternative Policies*

It is clear that the monetary policies followed from 1929 to 1933 were not the inevitable result of external pressure. At all times, alternative policies were available and were being seriously proposed for adoption by leading figures in the System. At all times, the System was technically in a position to adopt the alternative policies.

To give a clearer idea of the consequences of the policies actually followed, we consider explicitly the alternatives available at three critical periods and what their effects might have been. The periods are: (1) the first ten months of 1930; (2) the first eight months of 1931; (3) the four months following Britain's departure from gold in September 1931. This is followed by an evaluation of the chief justification that has been offered by writers on Federal Reserve history for the policy actually pursued in late 1931 and early 1932, namely, that a shortage of "free gold" greatly inhibited use of the policy alternatives available to the System until the passage of the Glass-Steagall Act at the end of February 1932.

The successive banking crises which followed the first period and occurred during the other two were, as we saw in section 2, each more severe than the preceding. Measures that might have been adequate to cope with the earlier ones would have been inadequate for the later ones. On the other hand, as we shall see, the bond purchases actually made in the spring and summer of 1932, which did halt the decline in the stock of money but were inadequate to prevent a subsequent relapse some months after, would have been more than adequate to cope with the earlier crises. As so often in human affairs, a stitch in time saves nine.

[138] Notes, Vol. III, Jan. 16; Feb. 2, 6, 16, 27, 1933; Conversations, Vol. II, Jan. 18, 1933. Quotation from Notes, Vol. III, Feb. 16, 1933.

JANUARY 1930 TO END OF OCTOBER 1930

None of the arguments later advanced in support of the view that expansionary monetary measures by the Federal Reserve System might have been ineffective or undesirable applies to this period, as noted above. There was no sign of lack of confidence in banks by the public, or of unusual concern by banks about their own safety. Banks were using reserves to the full. Any increase in reserves probably would have been put to use in expanding the assets of banks. Expansionary measures offered no threat to the gold standard. On the contrary, the gold reserve was high and gold inflows persisted. Throughout the twenties, the System had been concerned that it held too large a fraction of the world's gold stock; the only problem about gold that evoked discussion in 1930 within the System was how to repel the flow. Finally, no serious monetary difficulties had yet arisen abroad.

To evaluate the possible quantitative effect of an alternative policy, let us consider what the effect would have been if the purchase program actually carried out in 1932 had been carried out in 1930 instead; that is, if the System had embarked on a program to raise its security holdings by $1 billion during the first ten months of 1930. From December 1929 to October 1930, if we adjust for seasonal effects, government security holdings actually rose by $150 million. If some $850 million additional government securities had been purchased, high-powered money, instead of declining by $160 million, would have risen by $690 million, all of which would have increased reserves, since during the first ten months of 1930 the public reduced its currency holdings. However, changes in other forms of Reserve Bank credit might have reduced the impact of the hypothetical additional purchase. From December 1929 to October 1930, bills bought fell by $110 million—from $240 million to $130 million—and bills discounted fell by $390 million—from $590 million to $200 million. The purchase of $850 million additional government securities would doubtless have produced an even larger decline in bills discounted and less certainly in bills bought, since banks would have used some of the funds to repay borrowings and there might have been a larger demand for bankers' acceptances. To make rather extreme allowance for such an effect, let us suppose that discounts and bills bought had each been reduced to $50 million. Even then, the effect of the purchases would have been a rise in Federal Reserve credit outstanding by $130 million instead of the actual decline of $490 million, and a rise in high-powered money by $460 million.

If the deposit ratios had behaved as in fact they did, the change from a decline in high-powered money of $2\frac{1}{2}$ per cent to a rise of $6\frac{1}{2}$ per cent would have converted the actual 2 per cent decline in the stock of money into a rise of 7 per cent. Under those circumstances, the deposit ratios might have altered in a direction to offset some of the hypothetical rise in high-powered money. But even very large allowances on this score would hardly change the general conclusion: a rise in the System's security holdings by $1 billion instead of $150 million in the first ten months of 1930 would have changed the monetary situation drastically, so drastically that such an operation was almost surely decidedly larger than was required to convert the decline in the stock of money into an appreciable rise.

The change in the monetary situation might have affected the gold movement, reducing the gold inflow or even converting it into a gold outflow. But it would have done that only by its effects on the trend of economic activity and on the state of the capital markets. Only if the change in the monetary climate had lessened the severity of the economic contraction and made the capital markets easier, would it have affected gold flows. But it is precisely the achievement of such results that would have been the aim of the alternative policies. Hence, a reduction in the gold inflow would have been a sign of the success of the alternative policy, not an offset to it.

The hypothetical purchase of government securities would have reduced in two ways the likelihood of a banking crisis like the one in the fall of 1930: indirectly, through its effect on the severity of the contraction; and directly, through its effect on the balance sheets of banks. The indirect effect would have improved the ability of borrowers to repay loans; the direct effect would have meant that bank reserves were rising sharply instead of staying roughly stable. It is impossible to say with any assurance that these effects would have prevented a banking crisis from occurring—though they might have—but it is certain they would have reduced the magnitude of any crisis that did occur and hence the magnitude of its after-effects.

The effects on the capital markets and the reduction in the drain of gold from the rest of the world would have had desirable effects abroad. Again, these might not have prevented the later financial difficulties entirely, but they certainly would have eased them.

JANUARY 1931 TO END OF AUGUST 1931

The early months of 1931 were the next crucial time for monetary policy. The banking crisis had died down, there were signs of returning confidence in banks and of improving conditions in business. We have already suggested (section 2) that a vigorous monetary push at that time might have converted the faint signs of recovery into sustained revival.

Let us suppose that actual policy to the end of 1930, including the first banking crisis, had been what it was, but that in the first eight months of 1931 the System had raised its security holdings by $1 billion instead of $80 million, after allowing for seasonal changes. During those eight months, currency held by the public rose by $370 million as a result of the internal drain on the banking system; bank reserves fell by $120 million. The difference between the rise in currency and the decline in bank reserves, or $250 million, is the amount by which high-powered money rose. The purchase of $920 million additional government securities, with no change in bills discounted or bills bought, would have raised high-powered money by $1,170 million instead, enough to meet the drain of currency that actually occurred and at the same time to increase bank reserves by $800 million. With such a sizable increase in their reserves, instead of a decrease of $120 million, banks would have been freed from the necessity of liquidating securities, and could have reduced their borrowing from the Reserve System, instead of increasing it by $40 million. The bond market would accordingly have been far stronger, bank failures would have been notably fewer, and hence the runs on banks milder if at all appreciable. In consequence, the drain of currency into circulation would have been smaller than it was and the increase in bank reserves would have been even larger than these figures suggest.

To put the matter as before, in terms of the effect on Federal Reserve credit—again assuming that bills discounted and bills bought would each have been reduced to $50 million—had the System bought an additional $920 million of government securities during the first eight months of 1931, Federal Reserve credit outstanding would have risen by $470 million instead of $40 million. High-powered money, under these circumstances, would have risen by $680 million or by 10 per cent instead of by 3½ per cent. Even if both the deposit ratios had fallen by as much as they did, the result would have been no change in the stock of money, instead of a decrease of 5½ per cent.

On this occasion, however, effects of the change in the monetary climate on the deposit ratios would clearly have enhanced rather than offset the expansionary effect of the hypothetical open market purchases. Depositors would have been far less eager to convert deposits into currency and banks, to strengthen still further their reserve position. Both deposit ratios would therefore have fallen less than they did. The second banking crisis might indeed never have occurred at all in such a changed monetary environment. Once again a $1 billion purchase program would have been much greater than needed to change drastically the monetary situation. But even if the second banking crisis had occurred, and even if it had been as severe as it was, the hypothetical open market operation would have completely eliminated its effect on the stock of money.

Again, the change would have produced a reduction in the inflow of gold and might have converted it into an outflow with a resulting easing of the financial difficulties in Europe. And again, this must be counted an achievement of the hypothetical purchase program and not an offset.

SEPTEMBER 1931 TO END OF JANUARY 1932

We cited earlier the statement in a System memorandum written in November 1931 that the "foreign and domestic drain upon bank reserves [after Britain's departure from gold] were met in the classic way by increases in discount rates combined with a policy of free lending." The memorandum included a quotation from the *locus classicus* of central bank policy, Bagehot's *Lombard Street*. In fact, however, the System followed Bagehot's policy only with respect to the external drain, not the internal drain. To meet an external drain, Bagehot prescribed a high Bank rate, the part of his prescription the System followed. To meet an internal drain, he prescribed lending freely. "A panic," he wrote, "in a word, is a species of neuralgia, and according to the rules of science you must not starve it. The holders of the cash reserve must be ready not only to keep it for their own liabilities, but to advance it most freely for the liabilities of others."[139] Despite the assertion to the contrary in the memorandum, the System gave little more than lip service to this part of Bagehot's prescription, either before the external drain or after it ended. True, during the height of the internal and external drain in October, it permitted its discounts and its bills bought to rise sharply. But this was at the initiative of the member banks, in spite of sharp rises in the rates on both, and was a result of the desperate situation of member banks because of the double drain. As we have seen, even after the height of the crisis, the New York Bank reduced bill buying rates only gradually and kept them above market rates, so bills bought declined rapidly. The System took no active measures to ease the internal drain, as it could have done through open market purchases. Contrast its behavior with that reported approvingly by Bagehot:

The way in which the panic of 1825 was stopped by advancing money has been described in so broad and graphic a way that the passage has become classical. "We lent it," said Mr. Harman on behalf of the Bank of England, "by every possible means and in modes we have never adopted before; we took in stock on security, we purchased Exchequer bills, we made advances on Exchequer bills, we not only discounted outright, but we made advances on the deposit of bills of exchange to an immense amount, in short, by every possible means consistent with the safety of the Bank, and we were not on some occasions over-nice."[140]

Though the response of the System to the external drain was "classic," it was sharply at variance with the alternative policy the System had de-

[139] Walter Bagehot, *Lombard Street*, London, Henry S. King, 1873, p. 51.
[140] *Lombard Street*, pp. 51–52.

veloped during the 1920's, the gold sterilization policy. That policy called not for tightness but for ease to counter the gold drain and, even more clearly, for ease in the period before and after the gold drain to counter the internal drain.[141]

The System had sterilized inflows and outflows of gold during the twenties. It had more than sterilized inflows from August 1929 to August 1931. Consistent policy called for sterilizing the outflow after September 1931 as well. And the System was in an extraordinarily strong technical position to follow such a policy. Just before Britain's departure from the gold standard, the U.S. gold stock was at its highest level in history, over $4.7 billion, and amounted to about 40 per cent of the world's monetary gold stock. The System's reserve percentage—the ratio of its gold holdings to its note and deposit liabilities—exceeded 80 per cent in July, averaged 74.7 in September, and never fell below 56.6 in October. At the lowest point, toward the end of October, its gold reserves exceeded legal requirements for cover by more than $1 billion.[142] And this sum could have been expanded under pressure by $80 million to $200 million by simple bookkeeping adjustments.[143] Further, the Reserve Board had the legal power to suspend gold reserve requirements with negligible sanctions, a power it did in fact invoke in early 1933.

The major short-term balances subject to withdrawal were held by France. French short-term balances, which had been declining since 1929, amounted to $780 million in January 1931 (out of a total of $1.8

[141] For example, see the memorandum by Benjamin Strong, listing the reasons for the Federal Reserve easy-money policy of 1924, one of which was, "To check the pressure on the banking situation in the West and Northwest and the resulting failures and disasters. . ." (*Stabilization,* Hearings before the House Banking and Currency Committee, 69th Cong., 1st sess., Mar.–June 1926; Feb. 1927, pp. 335–336). One of the tests of Federal Reserve policy, 1922–26, that Strong proposed was the number of bank failures (p. 476). See also Adolph Miller of the Federal Reserve Board on the role of the System in lending to "banks that are in distressed communities" and supplying emergency currency needs (pp. 861, 898–899); and W. R. Burgess, then assistant Federal Reserve agent of the New York Bank, on the powers of the System for stabilization, including "desperate remedies for a desperate emergency" (p. 1019).

[142] In contrast, the System's gold reserve ratio was only 53 per cent at its maximum in 1919 when it permitted inflation to proceed unchecked, and it did not take contractionary action in 1920 until the ratio had fallen to less than 43 per cent.

[143] Federal Reserve notes in vaults of issuing Federal Reserve Banks were subject to the same collateral and reserve requirements as notes in circulation. On Oct. 31, 1931, there were about $320 million of such notes in vaults of issuing Banks. According to an internal System memorandum, about $120 million in vault would have been adequate (Harrison, Miscellaneous, Vol. I, enclosure, dated Aug. 20, 1931, in letter, dated Aug. 21, Harrison to McDougal). A reduction of $200 million would have released $80 million in required gold reserves held against the notes. If, instead of 60 per cent eligible paper, gold were held as collateral against the notes, an additional $120 million in gold would have been released from legal requirements.

billion held by European countries) and by September were around $700 million.[144] France was strongly committed to staying on gold, and the French financial community, the Bank of France included, expressed the greatest concern about the United States' ability and intention to stay on the gold standard. That accounted for the special volatility of the French balances. As it happened, though the French balances were not withdrawn in October 1931,[145] they were almost entirely withdrawn in the

---

[144] *Banking and Monetary Statistics,* p. 574. These are estimates of short-term balances held by France and all of Europe in reporting New York banks on Jan. 31, 1931. The peak figures a year earlier were $890 million and $2.0 billion, respectively.

[145] Harrison informed the Bank of France in Oct. that, if it did not want to invest its funds in the U.S. money market, he preferred not to hold French deposits in excess of $200 million. He suggested that it buy gold which would be either earmarked for the Bank of France or exported to France. The French representatives expressed surprise at Harrison's willingness to part with gold, but were not eager to withdraw it at the time because of their fears of possible inflationary effects of gold imports on the French economy and because of the loss of earnings to the Bank of France. It was agreed, however, that the Bank of France would effect a gradual repatriation of a substantial fraction of its balances in New York (Harrison, Notes, Vol. II, Oct. 15 and 26, 1931).

Rumors about Harrison's conversations with the French misrepresented their substance: he was said to have requested them not to take more gold from this country and they had not agreed; and he was said to have committed himself to maintain a firm money policy. He denied these rumors in a letter to Governor Meyer:

> I have reviewed these matters in some detail only because of the continued and repeated reports of an agreement in the nature of a "bargain" whereby the Federal Reserve Bank of New York surrendered its freedom of action regarding credit or discount rate policies in exchange for a promise from the Bank of France that it would not withdraw its funds from the market. There was not any such agreement, nor any such bargain. The Bank of France is perfectly free at any time it chooses to withdraw its dollar funds. The Federal Reserve Bank of New York is equally free in its credit and discount policies. In fact, there has never been a time in any of my conversations with any central bank when there was any request or even any suggestion that they or we should in any way make a commitment as to any future policy that would in any way destroy or limit our complete freedom of action in our own self-interest.

These statements by Harrison are not necessarily inconsistent with the assertion by E. A. Goldenweiser, who was director of the Board's Division of Research and Statistics at the time: "The Bank of France at that time had large deposits in the United States and it was understood by the authorities that, if bill rates in this country did not advance, these deposits would be withdrawn in gold."

Without France's asking for a commitment and without Harrison's entering into one, the French representatives could still have made it clear that they would regard failure of the United States to raise discount rates as a sign that the United States was not serious about its announced intention to take whatever measures were necessary to stay on the gold standard (Harrison, Miscellaneous, Vol. I, letter, dated Dec. 18, 1931, Harrison to Meyer; *ibid.,* letter, dated Dec. 22, 1931, Harrison to Calkins, who evidently had accepted the rumors as truth; E. A. Goldenweiser, *American Monetary Policy,* New York, McGraw-Hill, 1951, pp. 158–159).

spring of 1932.[146] Their withdrawal in October would have made no ultimate difference in the gold position. It would, however, have reduced the System's reserve percentage to about 49 per cent and hence might have had psychological effects somewhat different from those experienced when the balances were actually withdrawn, since the System's reserve percentage did not then fall below 58 per cent. The lowest the reserve percentage ever reached during the 1932 open market operation was 56 per cent (monthly averages of daily figures). Consequently, it seems highly likely that, if a gold sterilization policy had been adopted, gold outflows would have ceased long before the legal reserve ratio was reached, let alone before the gold stock was drastically depleted.[147]

Suppose the System had raised discount rates when it did, adopting the "classic" remedy for an external drain, but had accompanied the measure by purchase of government securities as called for by the "classic" remedy for an internal drain and by its earlier sterilization policy. Again, to be concrete, let $1 billion be the amount of the hypothetical increase in its security holdings. What would have been the consequence?

Between August 1931 and January 1932, currency held by the public rose by $720 million and bank reserves fell by $390 million, which means that, as a result of the increase in discounts and other minor changes, high-powered money had risen by $330 million despite the gold drain. Other items being the same, Reserve purchases of $1 billion of government securities would have meant an increase of $1,330 million in high-

[146] French short-term balances with reporting New York banks were, on selected dates, in millions: Sept. 16, 1931, $685; Dec. 30, 1931, $549; May 11, 1932, $304; June 15, 1932, $102; June 29, 1932, $49 (*Banking and Monetary Statistics*, pp. 574–575). The statistics include all deposits and short-term securities held by the French at reporting domestic banks and bankers, but they may not include other American short-term liabilities to French citizens, such as bills and short-term securities held for them by agents other than the reporting banks. Hence these figures may underestimate French withdrawals.

Governor Harrison denied that the ultimate withdrawal of French short-term balances reflected French dissatisfaction with the change in Federal Reserve policy in the spring of 1932, though that was widely reported. He said, "[S]ome people might argue that our policy had been responsible for the recent heavy outflow of gold, but we know that it was largely the repatriation of central bank balances which would have been withdrawn in any case" (Notes, Vol. II, June 30, 1932).

[147] Goldenweiser asserts the contrary, writing that "a full-fledged easing policy [by which he clearly means, from the context, low discount rates, rather than open market operations] . . . would have involved a suspension of reserve requirements against Federal Reserve deposits" (*American Monetary Policy*, p. 159). However, Goldenweiser gives no evidence to support his assertion. It may have been the opinion of the authorities at the time, though we have been able to find no internal document in the Goldenweiser Papers or in the Harrison Papers and no reference in the Hamlin Diary indicating that such a policy was ever seriously contemplated or its consequences for the reserve ratio explicitly considered. These documents make the rise in discount rates appear to be more nearly a conditioned reflex than a policy decision reached after full consideration of a range of feasible alternatives.

powered money. That sum would have provided the whole $720 million in currency withdrawn by the public and at the same time have enabled bank reserves to increase by $610 million instead of decreasing by '$390 million, or one-eighth of their initial level. The increase in bank reserves would have permitted a multiple expansion in deposits instead of the multiple contraction that actually took place.

Of course, under these circumstances, banks would have been under far less heavy pressure than they were and would have borrowed less from the Reserve System, thereby offsetting some of the hypothetical increase in high-powered money. However, this offset would have reflected fewer bank failures and a reduction in the public's desire to convert deposits into currency. Hence, the currency held by the public would have risen less than it did. The net effect of these offsetting factors on bank reserves might have been either expansionary or contractionary.

Again, to suggest orders of magnitude, suppose that from August 1931 to January 1932, discounts and bills bought had both remained unchanged instead of the first rising from $280 million to $840 million, and the second falling from $310 million to $100 million. Even under these assumptions, a purchase of $1 billion of government securities would have meant a rise in high-powered money by $650 million more than the actual rise. Even if we couple these assumptions with the further extreme assumption that, under such greatly improved monetary conditions, the deposit ratios would have fallen as much as they did—and for the deposit-currency ratio, the fall in so short a time was the largest on record—the result would have been to cut the decline in the stock of money to less than half the actual decline from August 1931 to January 1932. Only a moderate improvement in the deposit-currency ratio—a decline from 8.95 to 7.10 instead of to 6.47—would, under these hypothetical circumstances, have enabled the stock of money to be stable instead of falling by 12 per cent.

The crises were becoming successively more severe, so this time the $1 billion we have been using as our standard is not, as in the earlier periods, clearly a multiple of the amount required to turn the monetary tide. But these calculations suggest that an open market purchase of that size would have been adequate. And with so great a change in the monetary tide, the economic situation could hardly have deteriorated so rapidly and sharply as it did.

THE PROBLEM OF FREE GOLD

In the book he published after retiring from the System, from which we quoted above, Goldenweiser analyzed briefly the System's reaction to Britain's departure from gold. After discussing the rise in discount rates in reaction to the external drain, which he terms a "brief return to orthodoxy"[148] which "had only passing and temporary effects on the banking system or on the course of the depression," he went on to say, with respect to the internal drain:

More serious was the fact that the System did not extend sufficient aid to member banks through discounting their paper and that it failed to pursue a vigorous policy of purchases in the open market. For this failure of the System to give more help in an emergency the major blame is on the law which prescribed rigid rules for the eligibility of paper for discount and also barred government securities from collateral acceptable for Federal Reserve notes.[149]

The problem to which Goldenweiser referred is the so-called free-gold problem. The internal drain had increased the volume of Federal Reserve notes outstanding. The law specified that the System hold against notes a reserve of 40 per cent in gold and additional collateral of 60 per cent in either gold or eligible paper (which consisted of commercial, agricultural, or industrial loans, or loans secured by U.S. government securities rediscounted by member banks; loans to member banks secured by paper eligible for rediscount or by government securities; and bankers' acceptances, i.e., "bills bought" in the terminology of Federal Reserve accounts). Because the System did not have enough eligible paper to furnish 60 per cent of the collateral for Federal Reserve notes, part of the gold in excess of minimum requirements had to be pledged for this purpose. The amount of free gold not needed to meet either minimum gold requirements or collateral requirements was therefore less than the amount of excess gold reserves. The Federal Reserve System, in its *Annual Report* for 1932, and Goldenweiser, in the passage quoted above and elsewhere in his book, assert that the shortage of free gold was an important factor preventing the System from engaging in larger open market purchases, such as the hypothetical purchases discussed in the preceding subsection. Such purchases, they assert, would have reduced eligible paper holdings still further by reducing rediscounts and therefore could have been conducted only to a very limited extent without eliminating free gold entirely. The Glass-Steagall Act of February 27, 1932, disposed of that problem by permitting government bonds in the Reserve Banks' portfolios as well as eligible paper to serve as collateral against Federal Reserve notes in addition to the 40 per cent minimum gold reserve.[150]

Our own examination of the evidence leads us to a different conclu-

[148] However, while discount rates were raised at all Reserve Banks in Oct. or Nov. 1931, they were reduced a few months later only in Dallas and Richmond and New York. The reduction in New York was made more than four months after the second rise in Oct. 1931, and brought the discount rate only one-quarter of the way back to the level before the gold drain. Four months later, a second reduction was made in New York to 2½ per cent—only halfway back to the level before the gold drain—where the rate remained until raised again in March 1933.

[149] *American Monetary Policy*, pp. 159–160.

[150] See footnote 26, above, for other provisions of the Glass-Steagall Act.

sion. Despite the attention it has since received, we do not believe a shortage of free gold exerted any major influence on Federal Reserve policy, for five reasons.

(1) The earliest published full-dress discussion of free gold during the 1929–33 contraction we have found is an article by Benjamin Anderson in the *Chase Economic Bulletin* of September 29, 1930. Anderson, a firm believer in the real bills doctrine and an equally firm opponent of open market operations, warned, "There is not enough free gold to justify artificially cheap money."[151] We have found no evidence that the article exerted any influence within the Reserve System. In any event, by the time it appeared, New York had already lost its battle for expansionary open market purchases, and the general lines which were to dominate policy until the spring of 1932 had already been set.

(2) The earliest unpublished System document on free gold we have found is a memorandum by Goldenweiser, written on January 3, 1930. He refers to a Board discussion of a statement by Anderson "that free gold was down to $600,000,000 . . . " (in an address to the American Economic Association and American Statistical Association on December 30, 1929) ; Anderson concluded, "The Federal Reserve System is nearing the time when it must look to its own reserve . . . ." The memorandum makes clear that the Reserve System regularly kept track of free gold, and that its level was not at the time a source of concern to the Board.

The limited attention paid to free gold by the System is suggested by the fact that the earliest mention of free gold we have found in the Hamlin Diary is an entry of July 30, 1931, and in the Harrison Papers, a preliminary memorandum, August 3, 1931, for the meeting of the Open Market Policy Conference on August 11. Both noted that free gold on July 29 totaled $748 million and that internal bookkeeping adjustments, involving reduction of Federal Reserve notes in the tills of most Reserve Banks to a "reasonable minimum," would have raised the free gold on that date to $1,086 million.[152] A later memorandum of August 21, 1931, prepared at the New York Bank considered the likely effect on free gold of a variety of alternative hypothetical developments including large-scale open market purchases, internal drain of notes and gold, and an external drain and concluded that, even under rather extreme assumptions, free

---

[151] Anderson had referred to the significance of free gold in a Mar. 14, 1930, article (p. 13), indicating his intention to discuss the subject fully later, as he did in the Sept. 1930 *Bulletin* article, "The Free Gold of the Federal Reserve System and the Cheap Money Policy" (p. 8). W. R. Burgess told the Board that a subsequent article by Anderson on gold (*Chase Economic Bulletin*, Mar. 16, 1931) did much damage abroad to the Federal Reserve System (Hamlin, Diary, Vol. 19, Oct. 30, 1931, p. 173).

[152] See Goldenweiser Papers, Container 1, folder of Confidential Memoranda, 1922–33; New York *Times*, Dec. 31, 1929, which refers to Anderson's address; Hamlin, Diary, Vol. 19, p. 132; Harrison, Open Market, Vol. II.

gold did not constitute an important limitation on the alternatives available to the System.[153] The preliminary memorandum for the October 26 meeting of the Open Market Policy Conference noted there had been little change in free gold as a result of the gold outflow. Excess gold reserves had declined from $1.9 billion on September 16, 1931, to $1.1 billion on October 21, but free gold reserves had been roughly constant at over $0.8 billion because of a rise in eligible paper holdings. The preliminary memorandum for the November 30, 1931, meeting did not even refer to free gold, though it did note, "there is still plenty of gold left." After the first of the year, free gold may have fallen as low as $400 million during January and February 1932, which could have been raised to perhaps $525 million by bookkeeping adjustments.[154] Hence the actual amount of free gold throughout the whole period was sufficient to have permitted extensive open market operations.

(3) While free gold was alluded to from time to time at meetings of the Conference or of its executive committee or of the Federal Reserve Board or of the New York Bank directors, it was almost always mentioned as a problem by persons who had opposed open market operations all along on other grounds; it was never given as the principal argument against purchases, and the objections raised on this score almost always were immediately countered by figures showing that a shortage of free gold offered no serious limitation to policy.[155] It is impossible to read

[153] In his letter transmitting the memorandum to all governors, Harrison concluded, "apart from the position of individual Reserve banks the system as a whole has ample funds to deal with any situation within reason which may arise, and that in matters of policy we are probably in a position to do whatever seems wise for the country's economy."

The memorandum stated the immediate effect of the purchase of $300 million of government bonds would be a reduction of about $137 million in free gold, leaving the System about $600 million, which could be increased to more than $900 million by reducing Federal Reserve notes in vaults of the Reserve Banks. A large increase in the demand for Federal Reserve notes or for gold, according to the statement, would not affect the free gold position because that increase would be accompanied by an increase in Federal Reserve discounts and bill holdings, which would supply eligible paper collateral for Federal Reserve notes and release gold used for that purpose. Gold then in use as collateral, exclusive of free gold, was sufficient to provide a 40 per cent reserve for more than $3 billion of additional note circulation, or to provide $1¼ billion of gold for export (Miscellaneous, Vol. I).

[154] Open Market, Vol. II. No continuous figures on free gold during the critical period, Sept. 1931–Feb. 1932, were shown either in the *Annual Report* or *Federal Reserve Bulletin* for 1931 and 1932, and we have been able to find none in any System publication since. Our estimates for Jan. and Feb. 1932 are based on a chart in Federal Reserve Board, *Annual Report* for 1932, p. 17, plus amounts of their own notes held by issuing Banks, p. 91.

[155] At the Aug. 11, 1931, meeting of the Open Market Policy Conference, Governors Calkins and Seay said, in response to Harrison's recommendation of substantial purchases of government securities, their Banks did not hold enough free gold to permit them to participate in further purchases. Governor Harrison

in full the record of proceedings of the Open Market Policy Conference and of meetings of the New York Bank directors during the period from September 1931 through February 1932 and assign great significance to free gold as a factor determining policy. The closest approach to serious concern was expressed in January and February 1932, when the Glass-Steagall Act was in process of enactment and the problem was on its way to solution.[156] Concern over the gold problem during the period centered

---

cited the figures on free gold in the memorandum of Aug. 3, 1931, referred to above, and pointed out that "the question to decide was not whether individual banks could, or could not, participate, but to try to agree on a System policy which would be helpful." When the Conference met with the Board later that day, Governor Meyer asked if "there was any danger to the System" in authorizing the executive committee to purchase $200 million or $300 million of government bonds. "Mr. Goldenweiser stated that there was no danger in that direction as we have $750,000,000 free gold which can be increased to $1,000,000,000 by withdrawals from the agents" (Harrison, Open Market, Vol. II).

At a meeting of the executive committee of the directors of the New York Bank on Oct. 5, Owen D. Young asked how the purchase of government securities by the Reserve Banks "would fit into the proposed plan" for a corporation, eventually designated the National Credit Corporation. Harrison answered, "that he considered the gold position of the System paramount at this time, and on that account would not be inclined to purchase Government securities." Three days later, however, at a board meeting of the New York Bank, Harrison said "that the amount of free gold held by the System had not been materially affected by the recent loss of gold, so that there was still considerable leeway for purchases of Government securities" (Notes, Vol. II, Oct. 5, 8, 1931).

At the Oct. 26, 1931, meeting of the Conference, Harrison said that "the free gold position of the System was not a consideration at this time" (Open Market, Vol. II). On Oct. 27, Goldenweiser reported to the Board that free gold had been maintained despite the gold exports of the preceding five weeks (Hamlin, Diary, Vol. 19, pp. 169–170). No reference was made to free gold at the Nov. 30, 1931, meeting of the Conference, which authorized the executive committee to buy up to $200 million of government securities before the end of the year (Open Market, Vol. II).

The earliest mention of the free gold problem we have found in publications of the Federal Reserve Board is in the *Bulletin,* Sept. 1931, pp. 495–496. The term is defined and a chart is presented showing free gold and excess reserves of the Reserve Banks from 1925 on. It is referred to again in the *Bulletin,* Nov. 1931, p. 604. No mention of free gold is made in the *Annual Report* for 1931. In neither that report nor any earlier one is there a suggestion of legislation to meet such a problem, though it was standard procedure for the Reserve System to list legislative recommendations in its reports. The *Annual Report* for 1932, in commenting on the passage of the Glass-Steagall Act, contains the first discussion of free gold in the annual reports.

[156] On Jan. 4, 1932, Harrison told the executive committee of the New York Bank that "his only hesitancy in recommending" substantial purchases of government bonds "was on account of the relatively small amount of free gold "we now have at our disposal," and for that reason the Reserve Banks should have authority to pledge all their assets as collateral for Federal Reserve notes (Notes, Vol. II, Jan. 4, 1932).

His hesitancy did not prevent his urging open market purchases at the Jan. 11, 1932, meeting of the Conference (see sect. 5, above). At the Feb. 24 meeting just before the enactment of the Glass-Steagall bill, the System's failure to pursue

not in the Federal Reserve System but in the White House and Treasury. At a conference with Congressional leaders on October 6, 1931, President Hoover presented the proposals eventually embodied in the Glass-Steagall Act.[157]

(4) If free gold had been a serious handicap to a desired policy, feasible measures fully consistent with past policies of the System were available, even during the height of the gold drain, to relieve the free gold problem. (a) The bookkeeping adjustments referred to above were apparently exploited to some extent, but by no means fully. (b) Bills could have been purchased instead of government securities, since they were eligible as collateral for Federal Reserve notes. After rising sharply during the height of the crisis (September–October, 1931), holdings declined continuously from October 1931 to February 1932, because buying rates were kept above market rates.[158] (c) Member banks could have been encouraged

---

actively bill purchases, discount rate reduction, and "buying of Government securities, if necessary, facilitated by alleviation of free gold position," recommended on Jan. 11, was explained as follows:

> Continued uncertainties in the domestic situation, as well as a large drain of gold to Europe and particularly to France, stimulated by fear of inflation in this country, have been important factors in making it seem undesirable to carry through an aggressive program of reduction in discount rates and purchases of Government securities. The relatively small amount of free gold held by the reserve system was a further major factor in limiting the possibilities of purchases of Government securities (Open Market, Vol. II, minutes of meetings, Jan. 11, and Feb. 24, 1932).

[157] Hoover, *Memoirs*, pp. 115–118; see also Benjamin Anderson, "Our Gold Standard Has Not Been in Danger for Thirty-Six Years," *Chase Economic Bulletin*, Nov. 10, 1932, p. 10.

[158] On behalf of the System it could be claimed that the decline was not its own choice, that its buying rate on acceptances was below the rediscount rate, but New York City banks, which alone had bills, were substantially out of debt to the Federal Reserve Bank of New York by Nov. 1931 and hence had no incentive to sell (H. H. Villard, "The Federal Reserve System's Monetary Policy in 1931 and 1932," *Journal of Political Economy*, Dec. 1937, p. 727). The crucial point, however, is the relation of the buying rate, not to the rediscount rate, but to the market rate. As Villard has pointed out, from Aug. 1931 through Oct. 1931, while the System's bill holdings were expanding, its buying rate was at or below the market rate; thereafter its buying rate was ⅛ to ¼ percentage point above the market rate (*ibid.*, pp. 728–732). If the Reserve Bank had lowered the buying rate, the New York banks would have sold their acceptances to it. The New York Bank was fully aware that the relevant consideration was the relation of the buying rate to the market rate and not to the rediscount rate, as its actions in Aug. 1929 show. On Jan. 21, 1932, Harrison told his board of directors, "[W]e should probably have lowered our bill rates because they [are] well above the effective market rates and our portfolio of bills [is] rapidly diminishing" (Harrison, Notes, Vol. II).

Benjamin Anderson, who argued that the availability of free gold was a constraint on Federal Reserve expansionary policies (which, as we have noted, he opposed), nevertheless denied that the Glass-Steagall Act was essential to

THE GREAT CONTRACTION

to increase their discounts. At all times there was ample eligible paper in the portfolios of member banks.[159] Goldenweiser and others recognize this but say that the only way to increase the amount in the hands of the Federal Reserve Banks would have been to sell bonds and thereby force member banks to discount.[160] They add, quite correctly, that such a step would have been deflationary. However, that was not the only way. Failure of banks to discount was partly a consequence of the long-standing Federal Reserve pressure against continuous borrowing. In 1929, the System went beyond that and resorted to "direct pressure" to dissuade member banks from discounting for particular purposes. It would have been easier to use direct pressure to persuade member banks in 1931 or

---

relieve the constraint. He listed alternatives available for increasing the supply of free gold similar to those listed in our item 4. Concerning 40 (b) he wrote:

> Moreover, it would have been very easy to increase the volume of open-market acceptances available for purchase by the Federal Reserve Banks, by concerted policy involving the coöperation of banks and great business corporations—a proposal of this sort was actually made by important industrial leaders ("Our Gold Standard Has Not Been in Danger," p. 9).

[159] See the figures on country and reserve city member banks' holdings of eligible assets, including eligible paper and U.S. government securities not pledged against national bank note circulation, on June 30 or at call dates, June 1926 through Dec. 1932, Federal Reserve Board, *Annual Report* for 1932, p. 126.

Holdings of eligible paper, including paper under rediscount, were four times as large as member bank borrowings, when this ratio was at a low point in Dec. 1931. Of course, member bank borrowings were secured by U.S. government securities as well as by eligible paper, so the possibility of increased borrowing on the basis of eligible paper holdings in Dec. 1931 is understated.

On Mar. 24, 1932, in Hearings before the Senate Committee on Banking and Currency on S. 4115 (*National and Federal Reserve Banking System*, 72d Cong., 1st sess., p. 109), Senator Glass remarked, "Let me say that in an interview I had with him as late as last Saturday evening, the chief of banking operations in the Federal reserve system stated to me that the banks had ample eligible paper."

Holdings of eligible paper were also widely distributed, according to figures Glass presented during the Senate debate on the Glass-Steagall bill. He said he supported the section of the bill that permitted banks without eligible paper to rediscount other security satisfactory to the Reserve Banks, not because banks no longer held adequate amounts of eligible paper, but because of the psychological effect of the measure in freeing the fear-ridden banks from their inhibition to rediscount the eligible paper they owned (*Congressional Record*, Senate, Feb. 17, 1932, p. 4137; see also H. P. Willis and J. M. Chapman, *The Banking Situation*, New York, Columbia University Press, 1934, pp. 678–679).

[160] Goldenweiser, *American Monetary Policy*, p. 160; and Federal Reserve Board, *Annual Report* for 1932, p. 18. Benjamin Anderson believed force would not have been necessary:

> They [the Federal Reserve Banks] could have done this [sold government securities] without force, by arrangement with the great banks of the country in such a way as to tighten money markets little, if at all, if it were done in concert and as a matter of general policy ("Our Gold Standard Has Not Been in Danger," p. 9).

109

1932 to increase their discounts, since that could have been made profit-able for member banks.[161]

(5) Finally, enactment of the Glass-Steagall Act on February 27, 1932, entirely removed the problem of free gold. Yet, as we have seen, its enactment did not lead to a change in Federal Reserve policy. The large-scale open market operation of 1932 was begun six weeks later primarily because of Congressional pressure and was allowed to lapse not long after Congress adjourned.

The conclusion seems inescapable that a shortage of free gold did not in fact seriously limit the alternatives open to the System. The amount was at all times ample to support large open market purchases. A shortage was an additional reason, at most, for measures adopted primarily on other grounds. The removal of the problem did not of itself lead to change of policy. The problem of free gold was largely an ex post justification for policies followed, not an ex ante reason for them.

---

[161] The System need only have offered to discount member bank paper backed by government securities (which constituted acceptable collateral for Federal Reserve notes) at a rate below the market yield on government securities. Under Secretary of the Treasury Mills apparently made that recommendation to the Open Market Policy Conference meeting on Jan. 11 and 12, 1932. The Treasury, which had to raise $1½ billion by June 30, wanted to encourage bank subscriptions in the face of a severe depreciation in government securities since Sept. 1931. "The inclination of banks to subscribe would be increased by reduction of Federal reserve discount rates to give some differential between those rates and the yields on government securities. If banks can be induced to borrow and buy the net effect must be an expansion of credit" (Harrison, Open Market, Vol. II). No action was taken on the recommendation.

Suggestion of a "variation of the 'direct pressure' method, tried unsuccessfully in 1929," namely, "borrowing . . . would not be frowned upon by the Federal Reserve Banks," was made in 1930 by a New York Bank director, but it was not considered to be a practical solution of the problem (Notes, Vol. 1, May 26, 1930). Individual Reserve Banks must have differed at any given time in the encouragement to discount they gave their member banks. See, for example, Charles E. Mitchell's comments on the San Francisco Bank, which suggest that it was not liberal in its interpretation of eligibility requirements (Notes, Vol. II, Oct. 15, 1931). Even Harrison, who in Oct. 1931 recommended that New York City banks borrow freely from the System "what was necessary to meet the needs of the situation," hesitated to call bankers in to see him in this connection, because "we must be prepared to have our action construed as an invitation to come in and borrow from this bank and to do something with the funds thus obtained. This procedure would, therefore, have its responsibilities." Owen D. Young said he wanted "to stop, look, and listen," before proceeding "by calling group meetings of bankers and by issuing what will be, in effect, an invitation to the member banks to come in and borrow at this bank" (Notes, Vol. II, Oct. 26, 1931; Mar. 24, 1932).

Clark Warburton maintains that, far from encouraging discounting as a means of getting more eligible paper, "as bank failures became frequent, the Federal Reserve banks developed an extremely hard-boiled attitude toward member banks which needed to borrow to meet deposit withdrawals" ("Has Bank Supervision Been in Conflict with Monetary Policy?", *Review of Economics and Statistics*, Feb. 1952, pp. 70–71).

7. Why Was Monetary Policy So Inept?

We trust that, in light of the preceding sections of this chapter, the adjective used in the heading of this one to characterize monetary policy during the critical period from 1929 to 1933 strikes our readers, as it does us, as a plain description of fact. The monetary system collapsed, but it clearly need not have done so.

The actions required to prevent monetary collapse did not call for a level of knowledge of the operation of the banking system or of the workings of monetary forces or of economic fluctuations which was developed only later and was not available to the Reserve System. On the contrary, as we have pointed out earlier, pursuit of the policies outlined by the System itself in the 1920's, or for that matter by Bagehot in 1873, would have prevented the catastrophe. The men who established the Federal Reserve System had many misconceptions about monetary theory and banking operations. It may well be that a policy in accordance with their understanding of monetary matters would not have prevented the decline in the stock of money from 1929 to the end of 1930.[162] But they under-

[162] For example, H. Parker Willis, who played a major role in the evolution of the Federal Reserve Act, was regularly reported in the columns of the *Commercial and Financial Chronicle* in 1931 and 1932—he had resigned from the editorship of the *Journal of Commerce* in May 1931—as inveighing against open market operations and arguing that the only task of the Reserve System was to discount eligible paper. A cabled article by Willis in a French publication (*Agence Économique et Financière*) in Jan. 1932, announcing that the Federal Reserve System had adopted inflationary policies, created a sensation in European financial circles. Governor Moret of the Bank of France cabled the article to Harrison for comment. It read in part:

> Inflation is the order of the day . . . . The discount rate will probably be lowered at the next meeting of the Board of Directors of the Federal Reserve Bank of New York. [The rate was not lowered until Feb. 26, possibly because of Willis' article.] The reduction of the buying rate for acceptances in the open market which took place on Tuesday [Jan. 12] is a preparatory measure to which the Federal Reserve Bank always has recourse in such cases. Financial circles consider it an indication of a change in monetary policy and expect heavy purchases of government securities, acceptances, and perhaps of other bills . . . . There is reason to expect that all attempts to curb inflation and hamper credit expansion based on long term paper will meet with general opposition. Inflationary ideas have seriously taken hold of many minds in financial circles . . . . Wall Street . . . hails inflation as assuring an upward movement of securities . . . . The greatest danger inheres in the risks to which the Federal Reserve Banks are exposed in connection with the various proposals for the broadening of their discount and loan operations . . . . In view of these developments certain observers remark that the gold export which ceased some time ago may easily begin again, the markets which permit the free export of gold having everywhere become very narrow (Harrison, Miscellaneous, Vol. II, Willis article, dated Jan. 13, 1932, quoted in full in cable, dated Jan. 15, 1932, Bank of France to Harrison).

Telephone calls and cable messages were exchanged by the New York Bank and the Bank of France before the excitement over Willis' article subsided (Conver-

stood very well the problem raised by a panic attempt to convert deposits into currency, and they provided ample powers in the act to deal with such a panic. There is little doubt that a policy based solely on a thorough perusal of the hearings preceding the enactment of the Federal Reserve Act and a moderately informed understanding of them would have cut short the liquidity crisis before it had gone very far, perhaps before the end of 1930.[163]

Contemporary economic comment was hardly distinguished by the correctness or profundity of understanding of the economic forces at work in the contraction, though of course there were notable exceptions. Many

---

sations, Vol. II, Jan. 14, 1932, dictated Jan. 20; Miscellaneous, Vol. II, cable, dated Jan. 15, 1932). New York City banks also received cables from their Paris agencies inquiring about the article. On Jan. 16, Harrison asked Senator Glass to use his influence to stop "Willis' rather steady flow of disturbing and alarming articles about the American position" (Miscellaneous, Vol. II).

Willis followed his former teacher J. Laurence Laughlin in his espousal of the "real-bills" doctrine (see Chap. 5, footnote 7). He applied those criteria to the operations of Federal Reserve Banks when he helped draft the Federal Reserve Act while serving in 1912–13 as an expert on the House Banking and Currency Subcommittee of which Carter Glass was chairman. After Glass became a Senator, Willis continued to be closely associated with him.

[163] See *Banking and Currency Reform*, Hearings before a subcommittee (Carter Glass, Chairman) of the House Banking and Currency Committee, 62d Cong., 3d sess., Jan. 7–Feb. 28, 1913; and *A Bill to Provide for the Establishment of Federal Reserve Banks*, Hearings before the Senate Banking and Currency Committee (R. L. Owen, Chairman), 63d Cong., 1st sess., Sept. 2–Oct. 27, 1913, 3 vols. In the House hearings especially, many witnesses showed clear understanding of the remedy for a liquidity crisis: cf. the testimony of Leslie M. Shaw, former Secretary of the Treasury, pp. 99–101; F. J. Wade, St. Louis banker, pp. 219–221; W. A. Nash, former chairman of the New York City Clearing House Association, pp. 338–339; A. J. Frame, Wisconsin banker, pp. 415–421. Frame did not favor establishing a reserve system; he urged extension of the Aldrich-Vreeland Act to state banks so they could "obtain extra cash in time of trouble." If that were done, "we would never have a suspension of cash payments in the United States again" (p. 421). In the Senate hearings, cf. the testimony of G. M. Reynolds, Chicago banker, Vol. I, p. 228; and Nathaniel French, Iowa businessman, who testified, "We can prevent a panic such as occurred in 1907 . . . by provisions for an elastic note issue, the mobilization of reserves, and their use in time of need" (Vol. III, p. 2075).

Note also Clark Warburton's comment:

It is apparent that the Federal Reserve System could operate as intended—i.e., to provide an elastic currency without contracting member bank reserves—if and only if the Federal Reserve Banks acquired additional assets . . . to the full extent of increased currency issues in the form of Federal Reserve notes . . . . The necessity of keeping this principle in mind in the operations of the Federal Reserve System is so obvious—in view of its discussion in the literature preceding establishment of the Federal Reserve System and the provisions of the Federal Reserve Act—that the failure of Federal Reserve officials to handle the System in conformity with it in the 1930's warrants a charge of lack of adherence to the intent of the law ("Monetary Difficulties and the Structure of the Monetary System," *Journal of Finance*, Dec. 1952, p. 535).

professional economists as well as others viewed the depression as a desirable and necessary economic development required to eliminate inefficiency and weakness, took for granted that the appropriate cure was belt tightening by both private individuals and the government, and interpreted monetary changes as an incidental result rather than a contributing cause.[164]

The banking and liquidity crisis must, however, be distinguished from the contraction in general. It was a much more specific phenomenon, with far more clearly etched predecessors which had been studied and classified at length. One might therefore have expected a much better understanding of the banking and liquidity crisis and of the measures required to resolve it satisfactorily than of the contraction in general. To some extent, this expectation was fulfilled. For example, Congressman A. J. Sabath of Illinois wrote to Eugene Meyer in January 1931, after Meyer had turned down his suggestion that the proper response to the increase in bank failures was relaxation of eligibility requirements in order to encourage rediscounting: "Does the board maintain there is no emergency existing at this time? To my mind if ever there was an emergency, it is now, and this, I feel, no one can successfully deny. For while 439 banks closed their doors in 1929, during the year 1930, 934 banks were forced to suspend business." On the floor of the House, Sabath said, "I insist it is within the power of the Federal Reserve Board to relieve the financial and commercial distress."[165] Some academic people,

---

[164] See, for example, Alvin H. Hansen, *Economic Stabilization in an Unbalanced World,* New York, Harcourt, Brace, 1932, pp. 377–378. The repeated attempts to curb federal expenditures and the sharp tax rise in 1932 testify to the effectiveness of these views. Writing in 1932, A. B. Adams (*Trends of Business, 1922–1932,* New York, Harper, 1932, p. 68) stated:

> It would be quite undesirable to have an additional inflation of bank credit in this country at the present time. There is too much of the old inflation to be gotten rid of before business can be put on a sound basis. Temporary inflation would result only in a postponement of the inevitable deflation and readjustment and thereby result only in prolonging the present depression.

[165] *Reconstruction Finance Corporation,* Hearings before the House Banking and Currency Committee, 72d Cong., 1st sess., Jan. 6, 1932, pp. 78, 102–104. See also the testimony in March 1932 of former Senator R. L. Owen of Oklahoma, a banker and lawyer before his election to the Senate in 1907, and chairman of the Senate Banking and Currency Committee when the Federal Reserve Act was passed:

> The powers of the Federal Reserve Board and of the Federal reserve banks were abundantly great to have checked the collapse of values if they had had the vision to employ the authority given by law.
> Instead of expanding their credit when credit was being contracted and correcting the dangerous evil they contracted their own credits from December, 1929, to June, 1930, about $700,000,000 and only expanded it by Federal reserve notes when the depositors in banks were driven by fear to wholesale hoarding in August, 1930. Since January, 1932, they are again contracting credit.
> Clearly what the authorities of the Federal Reserve System should have done was to buy United States bonds and bills in the open market and emit Federal

such as Harold Reed, Irving Fisher, J. W. Angell, and Karl Bopp expressed similar views.[166]

Despite these important exceptions, the literature, and particularly the academic literature, on the banking and liquidity crisis is almost as depressing as that on the contraction in general. Most surprisingly, some of those whose work had done most to lay the groundwork for the Federal

---

reserve notes to the extent necessary to stop the depression as far as it was due to the contraction of credit and currency. They were so advised by the experts of the Royal Bank of Canada and by others. They should have needed no advice for a remedy so self-evident (*Stabilization of Commodity Prices,* Hearings before the House Subcommittee on Banking and Currency, 72d Cong., 1st sess., part 1, p. 136).

See also testimony of D. H. Fisher, a director of the largest national farm loan association in the U.S., and of an Indiana county bankers' association (*ibid.,* pp. 289–293).

The monthly letter of the Royal Bank of Canada noted in July 1932:

. . . [I]t is obvious that the attitude of the Reserve System during 1930 and 1931 to credit contraction was passive . . . When hoarding set in [dated October 1930 by the letter], this further contraction of credit was only partly offset by the purchase of securities . . . [I]t is necessary for large surplus reserves to accumulate in order that the banks should feel that it is safe for them to pursue a more liberal policy with their clients. It is noteworthy that in relation to the violence of the great depression, there has been much less of an accumulation of surplus reserves than in previous periods.

[166] See footnote 51 above; also H. L. Reed, "Reserve Bank Policy and Economic Planning," *American Economic Review,* Mar. 1933 Supplement, pp. 114, 117 (he subsequently qualified his argument, on the ground that qualitative controls need to be supplemented by quantitative controls, in "The Stabilization Doctrines of Carl Snyder," *Quarterly Journal of Economics,* Aug. 1935, pp. 618–620); Irving Fisher, *Booms and Depressions,* New York, Adelphi, 1932, pp. 96, 106, 126–134, 148–152; and J. H. Rogers, who wrote, "For the failure to create . . . a basis for much-needed credit and price expansion, the Federal Reserve System is by many capable students of its policy being held directly responsible. It is contended with much force that in periods like the present one, these central institutions must either use their great 'open-market' powers to arrest damaging price declines, or else must face highly deserved criticism" (*America Weighs Her Gold,* Yale University Press, 1931, pp. 206–209); W. I. King, who wrote, "Suppose . . . that in 1930, when prices began to plunge downward precipitously, the proper Federal authorities had begun vigorously to pump new money into circulation. Would not this process have started prices upward, restored confidence, or optimism, and brought business back to normal by the middle of 1931? The most probable answer . . . seems to be 'Yes!'" ("The Immediate Cause of the Business Cycle," *Journal of the American Statistical Association,* Mar. 1932 Supplement, p. 229); J. W. Angell, "Monetary Prerequisites for Employment Stabilization," in *Stabilization of Employment,* C. F. Roos, ed., Bloomington, Principia, 1933, pp. 207–214, 222–226; Karl Bopp, who wrote, ". . . Mr. A. C. Miller, who seems to be the dominant figure in the Board, has stated that he is opposed to open-market operations—the only effective method of stimulating revival from a severe depression—except as a 'surgical operation.' Even through 1932 he was not of the opinion that such a 'surgical operation' was necessary" ("Two Notes on the Federal Reserve System," *Journal of Political Economy,* June 1932, p. 390).

Reserve Act or who had been most intimately associated with its formulation—for example, O. M. W. Sprague, E. W. Kemmerer, and H. Parker Willis—were least perceptive, perhaps because they had so strong an intellectual commitment to the view that the Federal Reserve System had once and for all solved problems of liquidity. One can read through the annual *Proceedings* of the American Economic Association or of the Academy of Political Science and find only an occasional sign that the academic world even knew about the unprecedented banking collapse in process, let alone that it understood the cause and the remedy.

That climate of intellectual opinion helps to explain why the behavior of the Federal Reserve System from 1929 to 1933 was not checked or reversed by vigorous and informed outside criticism. But neither the climate of opinion nor external financial pressures nor lack of power explains why the Federal Reserve System acted as it did. None of them can explain why an active, vigorous, self-confident policy in the 1920's was followed by a passive, defensive, hesitant policy from 1929 to 1933, least of all why the System failed to meet an internal drain in the way intended by its founders. Economic contraction from 1929 to the fall of 1930, before the onset of the liquidity crisis, was more severe than it was from 1923 to 1924 or from 1926 to 1927. Yet, in reaction to those earlier recessions, the Reserve System raised its holdings of government securities by over $500 million from December 1923 to September 1924 and by over $400 million from November 1926 to November 1927 (all figures as of the last Wednesday of the month). By contrast, its security holdings in September 1930 were less than $500 million above the lowest level at any time in 1929 and more than four-fifths of the increase had occurred before the end of 1929 in response to the stock market crash. In the financially turbulent years, 1930 and 1931, the System's holdings of government securities varied over a narrower range than in all but two of the relatively tranquil years from 1922 through 1928—1925 and 1926.

The explanation for the contrast between Federal Reserve policy before 1929 and after, and hence for the inept policy after 1929, that emerges from the account in the earlier sections of this chapter is the shift of power within the System and the lack of understanding and experience of the individuals to whom the power shifted. Until 1928, the New York Bank was the prime mover in Federal Reserve policy both at home and abroad, and Benjamin Strong, its governor from its inception, was the dominant figure in the Federal Reserve System. Strong represented the System in its dealings with central banks abroad in a period when each of the great central banks seemed to be personified by a single outstanding individual—the Bank of England by Montagu Norman, the Bank of France by Émile Moreau, the German Reichsbank by Hjalmar Schacht. In the early years of the System, Strong was chairman and the dominant figure of the Governors Conference, a group composed of the chief executive officers of the twelve Reserve Banks. Later, in 1922, when the Conference established a Governors Committee on open market operations, out of which developed the Open Market Investment Committee, he was named permanent chairman.[167]

Strong began his career as a commercial banker. He had been deeply involved in the 1907 banking crisis, as secretary of the Bankers Trust Company, something of a "bankers' bank," and as head of a committee set up by the New York financial leaders "to determine which institutions could be saved and to appraise the collateral offered for loans."[168] That experience had greatly impressed him, as it did the banking community in general, and had given him a strong interest in the reform of banking and currency. It had much to do with his becoming the first governor of the New York Bank.

Strong, more than any other individual, had the confidence and backing of other financial leaders inside and outside the System, the personal force to make his own views prevail, and also the courage to act upon them. In one of his last letters on System policy, to Walter Stewart on August 3, 1928, he spoke of the necessity of an easy money policy to anticipate the approach of the "breaking point" Stewart feared, and commented:

Here is where I fear the consequences of hesitation or differences of opinion within the System . . . . If the System is unwilling to do it, then I presume the New York Bank must do it alone, despite the tradition which we have helped to create and maintain, that no extensive open-market operations should be conducted by individual banks. An emergency presents the possible need for emergency measures.[169]

One of the directors of the New York Bank recalled in April 1932, when the System finally began large-scale open market purchases, that he had once asked Strong, "why the authority for Federal reserve banks to purchase Government securities had been inserted in the Federal Reserve Act and that Governor Strong had replied that it was in there to use. Governor Strong had said further that if this power were used in a big way, it would stop any panic which might confront us."[170] If Strong had still been alive and head of the New York Bank in the fall of 1930, he

[167] See Chandler, *Benjamin Strong,* pp. 41–53, 69–70, 214–215, and Chaps. VII–XI.

[168] Chandler, *Benjamin Strong,* pp. 27–28.

[169] Chandler, *Benjamin Strong,* p. 460.

[170] Harrison, Notes, Vol. II, Apr. 4, 1932. The director, Clarence A. Woolley, then asked why the open market purchases "could not have been done sooner." He said, "the national nervous system has now been subject to strain for 29 months whereas, in former periods of business depression, 5 or 6 months have sufficed to clear up the worst of the wreckage. Is the Federal Reserve System responsible for cutting off the dog's tail by inches?" Burgess pointed out that "the presence

would very likely have recognized the oncoming liquidity crisis for what it was, would have been prepared by experience and conviction to take strenuous and appropriate measures to head it off, and would have had the standing to carry the System with him. Strong, knowing that monetary measures could not be expected to produce immediate effects, would not have been put off the expansionary course by a temporary persistence of the decline in business activity.[171]

Strong became inactive in August 1928 and died in October of that year. Once he was removed from the scene, neither the Board nor the other Reserve Banks, as we have seen, were prepared to accept the leadership of the New York Bank.[172] Chandler says in his biography,

---

of the Federal Reserve System tended to extend both the period of stimulation and of depression of business activity" (*ibid.*).

[171] See the copy of a letter, dated at Colorado Springs, Aug. 26, 1923, from Strong to Adolph Miller, in the Goldenweiser Papers (Container 3, folder of Open Market Committee, 1923–52). Strong wrote in part:

> The phenomena of credit somewhat resemble some of the phenomena of tuberculosis, concerning which I can speak with some certainty. Any imprudence or excess by a T. B. sufferer will not show ill results often for weeks or months. Some unusual mental or physical effort starts a slight inflammation which gradually develops, causes a lesion, then later comes the temperature, pulse, cough, etc. In our operations, suppose the imprudence consists in selling 50 or 100 millions of our Section 14 investments in the New York market . . . . [W]e can if we are ignorant or careless pull down the credit structure at a rapid and dangerous rate, by a sale of investments, which shortly causes pressure to liquidate a much greater volume of bank loans. That process is at maximum— (with rapid pulse and high temperature)—at some indefinite period following our sale, and we may fail to detect the cause on account of the lag I mention.

Irving Fisher said, "Governor Strong died in 1928. I thoroughly believe that if he had lived and his policies had been continued, we might have had the stock market crash in a milder form, but after the crash there would not have been the great industrial depression" (*Annals of the American Academy of Political and Social Science,* Philadelphia, 1934, p. 151). See also Carl Snyder, Capitalism *the Creator,* New York, Macmillan, 1940, p. 203.

[172] An episode in the struggle between the Board and the Banks, still earlier than the dispute about how to deal with the stock market boom, occurred in the fall of 1927, when the Chicago Reserve Bank was unwilling to reduce its discount rate in line with the easy-money policy originated by Strong and adopted by the Board. The Board finally ordered the Chicago Bank (by a 4 to 3 vote) to reduce its rate— an unprecedented action. The "action aroused bitter controversy both within and without the System . . . . Most of the critics questioned the legality of the action; all denied the wisdom of this assertion of power in the absence of an emergency." Though Strong himself wanted a reduction in the Chicago rate, he "was quite unhappy about the Board's action and sought to prevent, or at least to delay it" (Chandler, *Benjamin Strong,* pp. 447–448). Presumably, he saw the preservation of the Banks' independence and indeed dominance in the System as more important than the specific substantive action of the moment.

Governor Crissinger's resignation may have been related to that incident. The Board met on Sept. 9 to impose the rate without being informed by Crissinger that Strong had telephoned him earlier in the day asking him to delay the meeting until Secretary of the Treasury Mellon, who had conferred with Strong in New

Strong's death left the System with no center of enterprising and acceptable leadership. The Federal Reserve Board was determined that the New York Bank should no longer play that role. But the Board itself could not play the role in an enterprising way. It was still weak and divided despite the substitution of Young for Crissinger in 1927. Moreover, most of the other Reserve Banks, as well as that in New York, were reluctant to follow the leadership of the Board, partly because of the Board's personnel, partly because they still thought of it as primarily a supervisory and review body. Thus it was easy for the System to slide into indecision and deadlock.[173]

The Banks outside New York, seeking a larger share in the determination of open market policy, obtained the diffusion of power through the broadening of the membership of the Open Market Investment Committee in March 1930 to include the governors of all the Banks. Open market operations now depended upon a majority of twelve rather than of five governors and the twelve "came instructed by their directors" rather than ready to follow the leadership of New York as the five had been when Strong was governor.

The shift in the locus of power, which almost surely would not have occurred when it did if Strong had lived, had important and far-reaching consequences. Harrison, Strong's successor at New York, was a lawyer who had acted as counsel to the Federal Reserve Board from 1914 to 1920 before coming to the New York Bank as one of Strong's deputies. In 1929 and 1930, he operated in the aura of Strong's legacy and sought to exercise comparable leadership. As time went on, however, he reverted to his natural character, that of an extremely competent lawyer and excellent administrator, who wanted to see all sides of an issue and placed great value on conciliating opposing points of view and achieving harmony. He was persuasive yet too reasonable to be truly single minded and dominant. Nevertheless, if the composition of the Open Market Committee had not been changed, his policies might have prevailed in June 1930—though that change probably was partly a reaction to New York's independent actions to meet the stock market crash. As it was, he had neither the standing in the System nor the prestige outside the System nor the personal force to get his policy views accepted in the face of active opposition or even plain inertia. His proposals were repeatedly voted down by the other Bank governors. When they finally agreed to a large open market operation in the spring of 1932, they were halfhearted and only

York, upon his return from a trip abroad, would arrive in Washington the next day. Presumably Mellon would have tried to dissuade the Board from taking action, and in any case would have tied the vote (Hamlin, Diary, Vol. 14, Sept. 15, 1927, p. 38). Crissinger resigned Sept. 15.

[173] *Benjamin Strong,* p. 465. Hamlin, who resented the dominance of the New York Bank (see his Diary, Vol. 19, Aug. 10, 1931, p. 126), nevertheless wrote of Strong, "He was a genius—a Hamilton among bankers. His place will be almost impossible to fill" (Diary, Vol. 16, Oct. 18, 1928, p. 60).

too eager to discontinue it. On January 20, 1933, Harrison told Hamlin that a majority of the governors really favored a complete reversal of open market policy by letting government securities run off.[174]

We commented earlier on the difference in the level of understanding and sophistication about monetary matters displayed by New York and the other Reserve Banks. The difference is understandable in view of the circumstances in which the several Banks operated and of their responsibilities. New York was the active financial center of the country. The securities market in general and the government securities market in particular were concentrated there. So also were international financial transactions. New York was the only U.S. money market that was also a world market. Despite the attempt of the Federal Reserve Act to reduce the dominance of New York in the banking structure, the demands of banks in the rest of the country for funds continued to be channeled through the other Reserve Bank cities into New York, and banks in the rest of the country continued to maintain correspondent relations with New York banks, especially after the stock market boom got under way. The New York Federal Reserve Bank was therefore acutely sensitive to the state of the financial markets and to the liquidity pressure not only on banks there but also on their correspondent banks throughout the country. Among Reserve Banks, the New York Bank alone was effectively national in scope and accustomed to regard itself as shaping, not merely reacting to, conditions in the credit market. The other Banks were much more parochial in both situation and outlook, more in the position of reacting to financial currents originating elsewhere, more concerned with their immediate regional problems, and hence more likely to believe that the Reserve System must adjust to other forces than that it could and should take the lead. They had no background of leadership and of national responsibility. Moreover, they tended to be jealous of New York and predisposed to question what New York proposed.

The form which the shift of power took—from New York as dominant head of a five-man committee to New York as the head of an executive committee administering policies adopted by the twelve governors—also had an important effect. A committee of twelve men, each regarding himself as an equal of all the others and each the chief administrator of an institution established to strengthen regional independence, could much more easily agree on a policy of drift and inaction than on a coordinated policy involving the public assumption of responsibility for decisive and large-scale action.[175] There is more than a little element of truth in the jocular description of a committee as a group of people, no one of whom knows what should be done, who jointly decide that

[174] Diary, Vol. 22, p. 61.
[175] Compare statements by Harrison in footnotes 89 and 114 above.

nothing can be done. And this is especially likely to be true of a group like the Open Market Policy Conference, consisting of independent persons from widely separated cities, who share none of that common outlook on detailed problems or responsibilities which evolves in the course of long-time daily collaboration. Such a committee is likely to be able to take decisive action only if it happens to include a man who is deferred to by all the rest and is accustomed to dominate. Strong might have played such a role. Harrison could not.

The shift of power from New York to the other Banks might not have been decisive, if there had been sufficiently vigorous and informed intellectual leadership in the Board to have joined with Harrison in overcoming the resistance of some of the other Banks. However, no tradition of leadership existed within the Board. It had not played a key role in determining the policy of the System throughout the twenties. Instead, it had been primarily a supervisory and review body.[176] It had its way in early 1929 about the use of "direct pressure" instead of quantitative measures in dealing with speculation, because it had a veto power over discount rate changes, not because it was able to win the Banks to its views.

There was no individual Board member with Strong's stature in the financial community or in the Reserve System, or with comparable experience, personal force, or demonstrated courage. Roy Young, governor of the Reserve Board until September 1, 1930, was apparently an able administrator, and Strong supported his appointment. However, he took a leading role in the conflict between the Bank and the Board and strongly opposed open market operations in government securities. He left the Board to become governor of the Reserve Bank of Boston, a position which enabled him to continue to exert his influence against the policy favored by New York—and perhaps not less effectively than before. Young was succeeded by Eugene Meyer, who had left his Wall Street brokerage firm in 1917 to serve with a war agency, became head of the War Finance Corporation, and then served with a succession of government agencies, ending with the Federal Farm Board, before coming to the Reserve Board in 1930. Meyer was appointed just after Harrison had failed in his at-

[176] The salary structure in the System at that time is some indication of the relative position of the Banks and the Board and of their ability to attract able people. Board members received $12,000 a year until 1935. Though equal to the salary of cabinet members, those salaries were drastically lower than those of Bank governors (later presidents). Strong at New York received $50,000 a year from 1919 until his death, and Harrison the same. The salaries of other Bank governors ranged from a low of $20,000 (six southern and western Banks) to $35,000 (Chicago) during the twenties. The relative differentials were only slightly narrower in 1960: Board members, $20,000 (the chairman $500 more); the highest paid Bank president, $60,000 (New York); the lowest, $35,000 (all other Banks except Chicago and San Francisco).

tempt to persuade the other governors to engage in open market purchases and just before the onset of the first liquidity crisis—on both grounds a difficult time to get the System to change course sharply. Perhaps, if he had had more time to develop his leadership of the System, he might have been able to lead the System along a different route.[177] In the initial months at his post, he was in favor of expansionary measures and, through most of 1931, he tried unsuccessfully to persuade the Conference to approve larger open market purchases. During his six months as chairman of the RFC, February–July 1932, members of the Board felt he slighted his duties as governor. None of the other full-time members of the Board or staff had the personal qualities and the standing within the System to exercise the required leadership.[178]

[177] During Meyer's term of office, two committees of the Reserve System (including officials of several Reserve Banks), appointed to study problems of branch, chain, and group banking, and of reserves, submitted reports but no action was taken on their recommendations (see Report of the Federal Reserve Committee on Branch, Group, and Chain Banking, mimeographed, 1932; and "Member Bank Reserves—Report of the Committee on Bank Reserves of the Federal Reserve System," Federal Reserve Board, *Annual Report* for 1932, pp. 260–285). Meyer recommended to the Senate Committee on Banking and Currency a unified commercial banking system for the United States to be implemented by limiting banking privileges to institutions with national charters. He obtained the opinion of the Board's general counsel in support of the constitutionality of such legislation (*ibid.*, pp. 229–259), but no further steps were taken.

[178] Harrison opposed Meyer's acceptance of the chairmanship of the RFC (Notes, Vol. II, Jan. 21, 1932).

The remaining members of the Board from 1929 to 1933 consisted of Edmund Platt (who served as vice-governor until he left the Board on Sept. 15, 1930), Adolph Miller, Charles S. Hamlin, George R. James, Edward Cunningham (until Nov. 28, 1930), and Wayland W. Magee (after May 5, 1931). Platt had studied law, had been a newspaper editor, then a member of Congress (where he served on the Banking and Currency Committee) before he was appointed to the Board in 1920. Miller and Hamlin were members of the original Board appointed in 1914. Miller, an economist of considerable scholarly ability, had written some good articles on monetary matters. But he, and Hamlin as well, had already demonstrated just after World War I an incapacity to exert leadership and to take an independent course. In Chandler's words, Miller, "undoubtedly the most able of the appointed members of the Board, was the eternal consultant and critic, never the imaginative and bold enterpriser" (*Benjamin Strong*, p. 257, and also pp. 44–45). If any credence can be put in Hamlin's repeated comments on Miller, this is a generous evaluation. Hamlin's Diary makes Miller out to be a self-centered person, with little hesitancy in using his public position for personal advantage, and capable of shifting position on important issues for trivial reasons (see Vol. 4, Aug. 6, 1918, pp. 180–181; Vol. 6, May 6, 1921, p. 90; Vol. 14, Jan. 6, June 9, 1928, pp. 105, 106, 180; Vol. 16, Oct. 30, 1929, p. 194).

Hamlin was a lawyer, described by Chandler as "intelligent, . . . but . . . as one of his associates put it, 'an amanuensis sort of fellow unlikely to undertake anything on his own' " (*Benjamin Strong*, pp. 256–257). His Diary confirms this view. He was shrewd, particularly about political issues and details of administration, public spirited in a self-righteous way, dependable and honest, if inclined to be partisan, and, fortunately for our purposes, an inveterate and, so far as we can judge, an accurate gossip. But the Diary shows exceedingly limited under-

The detailed story of every banking crisis in our history shows how much depends on the presence of one or more outstanding individuals willing to assume responsibility and leadership.[179] It was a defect of the financial system that it was susceptible to crises resolvable only with such leadership. The existence of such a financial system is, of course, the ultimate explanation for the financial collapse, rather than the shift of power from New York to the other Federal Reserve Banks and the weakness of the Reserve Board, since it permitted those circumstances to have such far-reaching consequences. Nonetheless, given the financial system that existed, the shift of power and the weakness of the Board greatly reduced the likelihood that the immediate decisive action would be taken, which was required to nip the liquidity crisis in the bud.

In the absence of vigorous intellectual leadership by the Board or of a consensus on the correct policy in the community at large or of Reserve Bank governors willing and able to assume responsibility for an independent course, the tendencies of drift and indecision had full scope. Moreover, as time went on, their force cumulated. Each failure to act made another such failure more likely. Men are far readier to plead—to themselves as to others—lack of power than lack of judgment as an explanation for failure. We have already seen this tendency expressed in the

---

standing of the broader issues of monetary policy and no sign of venturesomeness in thought or action. James was a small merchant and manufacturer from Tennessee and, for a few years, had been president of a commercial bank; Cunningham, a farmer; Magee, also a farmer and rancher, who had been a member of the board of the Omaha branch of the Reserve Bank of Kansas City and then a director of the Bank of Kansas City (see Chandler's comments, *Benjamin Strong,* pp. 256–257).

Of the staff, E. A. Goldenweiser, director of research and statistics from 1926 to 1945, was perhaps the most influential, but he was primarily a technician. His predecessor, Walter W. Stewart, had been close to Strong, had influenced him greatly, and continued their relationship after leaving the Board in 1926. Goldenweiser was a gentle person who could not match Stewart's influence on policy.

The ex officio members of the Reserve Board were the Comptroller of the Currency, and the Secretary of the Treasury, who served as chairman—from 1921 to February 1932, Andrew W. Mellon, a well-known financier and industrialist at the time of his appoinment; thereafter, until March 1933, Ogden L. Mills. Mills, a lawyer, tax expert, and Congressman, before becoming Under Secretary of the Treasury in 1927, was an able and forceful man. As mentioned above, he gave active support to the Glass-Steagall bill because he saw lack of free gold limiting Federal Reserve action. Mills apparently contributed the chief ideas embodied in the Emergency Banking Act of Mar. 9, 1933 (see Chapter 8).

J. W. Pole, formerly chief U.S. national bank examiner, and Comptroller of the Currency from 1928 to September 1932, advocated as a bank reform measure branch banking limited to "trade areas" or regions around important cities. But he had no influence of record on bank legislation or Federal Reserve policy during that period (see Comptroller of the Currency, *Annual Report,* 1929, p. 5; 1930, p. 5; 1931, p. 1). Hamlin referred to him as "on the whole, a good but not very strong man" (Diary, Vol. 21, Sept. 1, 1932, pp. 105–106).

[179] See Sprague, *History of Crises, passim.*

Federal Reserve System's reaction to the criticism of its policies during 1919–21. It was expressed again in 1930–33 as the Board explained economic decline and then banking failures as occurring despite its own actions and as the product of forces over which it had no control. And no doubt the Board persuaded itself as well as others that its reasoning was true. Hence, as events proceeded, it was increasingly inclined to look elsewhere for the solution, at first to hope that matters would right themselves, then increasingly to accept the view that crisis and doom were the inescapable product of forces in the private business community that were developing beyond the System's control. Having failed to act vigorously to stem the first liquidity crisis in the fall of 1930, the System was even less likely to act the next time. It was only great pressure from Congressional critics that induced the System to reverse itself temporarily in early 1932 by undertaking the large-scale securities purchases it should have made much earlier. When the operation failed to bring immediate dramatic improvement, the System promptly relapsed into its earlier passivity.

The foregoing explanation of the financial collapse as resulting so largely from the shift of power from New York to the other Federal Reserve Banks and from personal backgrounds and characteristics of the men nominally in power may seem farfetched. It is a sound general principle that great events have great origins, and hence that something more than the characteristics of the specific persons or official agencies that happened to be in power is required to explain such a major event as the financial catastrophe in the United States from 1929 to 1933.

Yet it is also true that small events at times have large consequences, that there are such things as chain reactions and cumulative forces. It happens that a liquidity crisis in a unit fractional reserve banking system is precisely the kind of event that can trigger—and often has triggered—a chain reaction. And economic collapse often has the character of a cumulative process. Let it go beyond a certain point, and it will tend for a time to gain strength from its own development as its effects spread and return to intensify the process of collapse. Because no great strength would be required to hold back the rock that starts a landslide, it does not follow that the landslide will not be of major proportions.

Director's Comment

ALBERT J. HETTINGER, JR.

PARTNER, LAZARD FRÈRES AND COMPANY

THE National Bureau affords its directors the privilege of submitting a "memorandum of dissent or reservation" to a manuscript accepted for publication. What I am submitting are neither dissents nor reservations, but a questioning comment. I have read the manuscript twice, in original draft and in final galley proof. I eagerly await the more pleasant reading afforded by a published volume, where tables appear in context and charts, by their presence, remove that need for faith, defined by St. Paul as "the substance of things hoped for, the evidence of things not seen." This volume, if my judgment is sound, is one of the truly great ones published by the National Bureau. Its breadth of scope, its penetrating use of analytical tools to set forth, dissect, and in a sense reconstitute, as it might have been, nearly a century of the monetary history of the United States, has created a finished product that I will reread more than once with enjoyment coupled with a conviction that time so spent is profitably employed. My questioning is not of the logic of a brilliant presentation, but of an underlying assumption. My brief comments will be based largely upon the period 1929–33. The authors state, in their summation of the period, "There is one sense—and, so far as we can see, only one—in which a case can be made for the proposition that the monetary decline was a consequence of the economic decline. That sense is not relevant to our main task of seeking to understand economic relations, since it involves relying primarily on psychological and political factors" (p. 691).

We are inevitably, in varying degrees, influenced by our background and environment. Mine compels me to place much greater weight upon these "psychological and political factors" than the authors would be willing to concede. I am a businessman by profession, an amateur economist by avocation. My doctor's degree in economics regrettably lies nearly half a century in the past; my few years of university teaching are almost as remote; competitive business, a combination of industry and finance, has been my profession since 1926. To me, business is simply decision making and calculated risk taking. Decisions are not always easy, and the risk taking is real; I survive by virtue of my competitors' mistakes—if they did not make about as many as I do, I would be an ex-businessman. It has been burned in upon me that monetary policy, in final analysis, acts on men whose conduct is not predictable; it neither operates in vacuum nor in a world in which all other factors can be taken as constant.

The difficulty of predicting the impact of economic measures was faced in the *Third Report* of the British Council on Prices, Productivity and Incomes, generally assumed to have been written by Sir Dennis Robertson.[1] After some 72 sections attempting to analyze the situation and weigh the probabilities, there follows: "But no precise judgment of the balance of all these factors is possible; economic restraints and incentives operate on men's minds where it is not possible to forecast their precise effects; they operate also in circumstances which are constantly changing." And Lord Keynes, here a "decision maker," told the 1931 annual meeting of the investment trust of which he was chairman: "I have reluctantly reached the conclusion that nothing is more suicidal than a rational investment policy in an irrational world" (quoted from memory, without verification of exact phraseology). He also states in his *Treatise on Money:* "To diagnose the position precisely at every stage and to achieve this exact balance may sometimes be, however, beyond the wits of man."[2] One final example: Sir Henry Clay's biography of Lord Norman[3] tells of the head of the Bank of England, physically exhausted but feeling that the international monetary system was temporarily under control, yielding to doctors' orders and taking a brief cruise on the Mediterranean—to be greeted when the ship put into port with the news that Britain had gone off gold!

The authors of this volume in discussing the silver situation (1893–97) recognize the importance of psychological and political factors when they say, "the entire silver episode is a fascinating example of how important what people think about money can sometimes be. The fear that silver would produce an inflation sufficient to force the United States off the gold standard made it necessary to have a severe deflation in order to stay on the gold standard" (p. 133).

I have often wished that Professor Taussig had included, in the economic text I studied, a chapter on the force of momentum. Value, I was taught, was the determining long-run factor, and deviations in price from value, short term and self-correcting. I learned the force of a spiraling downward momentum, feeding on emotional fear, during the 1929–33 period, and experienced a replay during the confidence crisis and stock market debacle of the spring of 1962. A nonstatistical view

[1] London, H.M. Stationery Office, July 1959, p. 25, paragraph 73.
[2] New York, Harcourt, Brace, 1930, Vol. I, p. 255.
[3] *Lord Norman,* London, Macmillan, 1957.

of the psychology of the 1929–33 period was presented in a paper delivered by J. M. Barker (university teacher, banker, and senior official of Sears, Roebuck & Co.) before a midwestern conference of bankers in 1936, from which I quote:

> Whenever you have a group of people thinking the same thing at the same time you have one of the hardest emotional causes in the world to control. The more people that are thinking the same thing the more surely you are at the mercy of unreasoning, emotional mob psychology as a cause, with sometimes dire economic effects. . . . If you consider the universality of the speculative mania of the later days of the last boom, you will see how completely the people of this country, to say nothing of the world, were under the influence of the mob psychology of unreasoning, emotional cupidity. When the break came, cupidity turned into unreasoning, emotional, universal fear. . . . In every city of this country, business men, hard hit or already wiped out in the stock market in the earlier part of the crash, were still watching the quotations every day to see how things were going. They saw the market dropping, dropping, dropping. Is there any doubt they made their decisions from day to day under the influence of the emotional backgrounds formed by their observations of the falling security prices?

The authors are highly critical of Federal Reserve policies. The continuing conflicts within the system are convincingly documented: Board, Open Market Committee, and individual Reserve Banks—they call to mind the line from one of Ibsen's plays that runs: "When the devil decided that nothing be accomplished, he appointed the first committee." The authors' diagnosis: "The bull market brought the objective of promoting business activity into conflict with the desire to restrain stock market speculation. The conflict was resolved in 1928 and 1929 by adoption of a monetary policy, not restrictive enough to halt the bull market yet too restrictive to foster vigorous business expansion" (pp. 297–298). Their conclusion that "the Board should not have made itself an 'arbiter of security speculation or values' and should have paid no direct attention to the stock market boom" (p. 291) is one I am not sure I can accept. With holding company superimposed on holding company, call loans for "others" mounting by the billion, and momentum feeding on itself, the monetary ease that would have "fostered vigorous expansion" might well have cumulated economic maladjustments whose correction was merely postponed. As it was, when the break came, "as in pre-Federal Reserve times, J. P. Morgan and Company assumed leadership of an effort to restore an orderly market by organizing a pool of funds"—yet "by the second week after the crash the phase of organized support of the market was over" (p. 305). This was a different kind of depression.

With possibly unjustifiable oversimplification in description on my part, the basic weapon in the authors' arsenal may be termed their concept of high-powered money. Their treatment of its role is consistent and brilliantly analytical in depth. One point only disturbs me. There is no question as to the mathematical demonstration. If high-powered money could be increased by the Federal Reserve without that very move setting other forces in motion, unpredictable both as to source and intensity, I would have no reservations. I lack competence to pass judgment. This is not a controlled experiment, with high-powered money increased, and all other factors remaining constant. Depositors were watching their banks. "One of the reasons New York City banks were said to be reluctant to borrow from the Reserve Bank was the fear that Europeans would interpret borrowing as an indication of weakness" (p. 317). "The aversion to borrowing by banks . . . was still greater at a time when depositors were fearful of the safety of every bank and were scrutinizing balance sheets with great care to see which banks were likely to be next to go" (p. 318). To borrow from the RFC was the kiss of death: "the inclusion of a bank's name on the list was correctly interpreted as a sign of weakness, and hence frequently led to runs on the bank" (p. 325). It is difficult today to recall "the dominant importance then attached to the preservation of the gold standard and the greater significance attached to external than to internal stability, by both the System and the community at large" (p. 363). Summarizing, in the words of Lord Keynes: "If we are dealing with a closed system, so that there is only the condition of internal equilibrium to fulfill, an appropriate banking policy is always capable of preventing any serious disturbance to the *status quo* from developing at all. . . . But when the condition of external equilibrium must also be fulfilled, then there will be no banking policy capable of avoiding disturbance to the internal system."[4] A parallel reading of Professor Chandler's biography of Benjamin Strong[5] and that of Lord Norman by Sir Henry Clay should leave no doubt that we were dealing with no closed system; the extent of the erosion of newly created high-powered money would be one measure of the "disturbance to the internal system" that I (with what justification I am not capable of answering) would not treat lightly.

The authors ask, "Why was monetary policy so inept?" and answer, "We trust that, in light of the preceding sections of this chapter, the adjective used . . . to characterize monetary policy during the critical period from 1929 to 1933 strikes our readers, as it does us, as a plain description of the fact. The monetary system collapsed, but it clearly need not have done so" (p. 407). The monetary policy certainly was unsuccessful, and probably the characterization of "inept" is justified. With respect to the final statement that the collapse of the monetary

[4] *A Treatise on Money,* Vol. I, p. 349.
[5] Lester V. Chandler, *Benjamin Strong,* Washington, D.C., Brookings, 1958.

system was unnecessary, this I cannot feel has been proved. To me, each move in the high-powered-money arsenal involves a calculated risk. If its impact on men's minds is favorable, possibly even if it is neutral, the arithmetical results postulated by the authors follow as night after day. I merely cite at this point the earlier quotation from the report of the British Council on Prices, Productivity and Incomes. If those moves were deemed inflationary and "unsound," the results could have been other than those desired. In that day a citizen fearing devaluation could choose gold rather than paper, and the international flow of gold, seeking safety, was as unpredictable as that of a gun loose on a battleship pitching in heavy seas. The authors may well be right; they are outstanding monetary economists—but I would prefer the terms "possibly" or conceivably "probably" rather than "clearly" need not have happened.

If my recollection is correct, the most striking illustration of the potentialities of high-powered money are those cited in connection with the five-month period ended January 1932, in which deposits fell by $5,727 million. "The provision of $400 million of additional high-powered money to meet the currency drain without a decline in bank reserves could have prevented a decline of nearly $6 billion in deposits" (p. 346). Mathematically this was possible. Reviewing the economy in the United States at that time, and the situation in both Britain and Central Europe, I cannot believe that what in theory "could" have happened, in actuality "would" have happened.

There is a well-documented analysis of what would have happened had one billion dollars of additional high-powered money been introduced into the economy during any one of three strategic periods in the great depression: (1) January 1930 to end of October 1930, (2) January 1931 to end of August 1931, and (3) September 1931 to end of January 1932. Were a Lloyds to underwrite the assumed potential turning of the tide, I could rest more easily. If it be permitted to lapse into the terminology of the market place, there is a vast difference between gross income and net income. This would be determined by the reaction on men's minds, not only in this country, but in every monetary center of the world. Had it been favorable, the authors' assumptions are tenable; had it, for instance, been deemed an inflationary threat to the gold standard, the "cost" (in erosion of those high-powered dollars) could have reduced the "net" to such an extent as would have precluded the results confidently anticipated by the authors. Again, I don't know; I am merely questioning.

In Kerrville, Texas, the "Bank of the Charles E. Schreiner Estate" is run by Louis Schreiner, aged about 90, and was founded by his father, old Captain Schreiner, as he is termed in those parts. The old Captain laid down the rule: "The time to call your loan is before you make it," and in almost a century, good times and bad, that bank has never called a loan. High-powered money, intelligently administered by a regulatory body, can, as the authors point out, accomplish much. It cannot accomplish the impossible—there seems to me an analogy in Lord Keynes' rueful remark: "Nothing is more suicidal than a rational investment policy in an irrational world." I would have more hope of its keeping us out of trouble than in its ability to turn an emotional tidal wave after we got into trouble.

I claim no validity for my "questioning comment." During my university days I would have placed little emphasis upon the psychological and political factors: a long life in business has changed my views. The story is told that Bismarck in council, after his staff had scoffed at certain factors which they termed imponderable, reached his decision: "Gentlemen, the Imponderables have it." I have no idea whether his decision was correct, and similarly I have no idea whether the weight I attach to imponderables has validity. My comments are set forth with humility, because I have made too many mistakes to do otherwise.

Over all, my admiration for *A Monetary History of the United States, 1867–1960* is unrestrained.

Glossary

BILLS BOUGHT represent bankers' and trade acceptances bought by Federal Reserve Banks from bill (acceptance) dealers and banks. The Reserve Banks generally buy all prime bills offered at the buying rates they establish.

BILLS DISCOUNTED represent the amount of Federal Reserve credit member banks obtain through borrowing from Reserve Banks. In 1929-33, two principal forms of borrowing, both known as discounting, were resorted to by member banks in order to maintain adequate reserves: (1) rediscounts of short-term commercial, industrial, agricultural, or other business paper in the member banks' portfolios; (2) advances to member banks on their own promissory notes, secured by paper eligible for discounting or by government securities.

CONTINUOUS ANNUAL RATE is a rate of change calculated by assuming continuous compounding. It is the difference between the natural logarithms of a variable at the terminal and initial dates divided by the number of years separating those dates.

DEPOSIT-CURRENCY RATIO is the ratio of commercial bank deposits to currency held by the public. The higher this ratio, the larger the fraction of high-powered money in use as bank reserves, and hence the larger the money stock, given high-powered money and the deposit-reserve ratio. The effect on the money stock of a change in this ratio depends on the size of the deposit-reserve ratio.

DEPOSIT-RESERVE RATIO is the ratio of commercial bank deposits to bank reserves. The higher this ratio, the larger the amount of deposits outstanding for a given amount of reserves. Any increase in the ratio of deposits to reserves tends to produce a drain of currency into public circulation, and hence changes the amount of reserves. The effect on the money stock of a change in this ratio, therefore, depends on the size of the deposit-currency ratio.

DIRECT PRESSURE, mentioned on p. 54, footnote 60, is explained on pp. 109-110.

FEDERAL RESERVE CLAIMS ON THE PUBLIC AND BANKS is the difference between Federal Reserve credit outstanding and Federal Reserve holdings of U.S. government securities.

FEDERAL RESERVE CREDIT OUTSTANDING represents principally the loans and investments of Federal Reserve Banks. It is the sum of bills bought, bills discounted, U.S. government securities, and other Reserve Bank credit.

FIAT OF THE MONETARY AUTHORITIES refers to the fiduciary contributions of the Federal Reserve System and the Treasury to high-powered money. High-powered money is a sum of Treasury obligations and Federal Reserve obligations. Against some of these obligations, the monetary authorities hold nonfiduciary assets, e.g., gold stock assets for gold certificates; Federal Reserve claims on the public and the banks, such as bills discounted or bills bought, for some Federal Reserve notes and bank deposits at Federal Reserve Banks. Against other obligations, the monetary authorities hold fiduciary assets, based on their fiat, e.g., Federal Reserve holdings of government securities for some Federal Reserve notes and bank deposits at Federal Reserve banks.

HIGH-POWERED MONEY is currency held by the public, plus vault cash in banks, plus deposit liabilities of the Federal Reserve System to banks. The total is called high-powered money because one dollar of such money held as bank reserves may give rise to the creation of several dollars of deposits. Other things being the same (namely, the deposit-reserve ratio and the deposit-currency ratio), any increase in the total of high-powered money involves an equal percentage increase in the stock of money.

IMPLICIT PRICES is the index of prices obtained by dividing net national product in current prices by net national product in 1929 prices.

MONETARY AUTHORITIES are government bodies that exercise ultimate power over the determination of the total amount of money in existence. The principal monetary authorities in the United States since 1914 have been the Federal Reserve System and the Treasury.

MONEY STOCK is the seasonally adjusted sum of currency and deposits at commercial banks held by the public; in present Federal Reserve terminology, it is the sum of currency outside banks, adjusted demand deposits, and commercial bank time deposits.

NET NATIONAL PRODUCT is used interchangeably with national income. The measure of net national product is variant III, computed by Simon Kuznets in *Capital in the American Economy: Its Formation and Financing*, Princeton for NBER, 1961.

PROXIMATE DETERMINANTS OF THE MONEY STOCK are the three major quantities we distinguish through which any changes in the stock of money (M) must, arithmetically, occur: (1) high-powered money

(H); (2) deposit-reserve ratio $\left(\dfrac{D}{R}\right)$; (3) deposit-currency ratio $\left(\dfrac{D}{C}\right)$. The formula connecting them with the money stock is

$$M = H \cdot \frac{\dfrac{D}{R}\left(1 + \dfrac{D}{C}\right)}{\dfrac{D}{R} + \dfrac{D}{C}} \cdot$$

See *A Monetary History*, Appendix B, for the reasons for selecting these three determinants and for the precise method used to divide a change in the money stock into the fraction attributable to each separately and to interaction between the two ratios.

RESERVES OF BANKS equal high-powered money held by commercial banks, and consist of vault cash in banks plus deposit liabilities of the Federal Reserve System to banks. It is not the sum of reserves as viewed by individual banks, which regard their deposits at other banks as reserves. It is the amount that would appear on a consolidated balance sheet of the commercial banks, in which interbank deposits cancel out.

VELOCITY is the ratio of net national product in current prices to the money stock. The money stock is the estimated average stock for the time unit (generally, a calendar year) to which the net national product refers.

Primary Sources

IN WRITING *A Monetary History,* we did not have access to the internal documents of the Federal Reserve System dealing with monetary policy. We were therefore pleased by the announcement, in August 1964, of the intention of the Board of Governors of the Federal Reserve System to make available to scholars most such documents covering the period 1914-60. These will make it unnecessary in future research to rely as heavily as we did on the following primary sources.

The Goldenweiser Papers. For a description of the papers and their author, see pp. 81-82, footnote 107, and pp. 121-122, footnote 178.

The Diary of Charles S. Hamlin. Hamlin was a Boston lawyer who was appointed to the Federal Reserve Board in August 1914 for a two-year term, and reappointed for ten-year terms in 1916 and 1926, serving until 1936, when he was appointed special counsel. He kept a detailed record of his daily round of activities, including proceedings of the Board.

The George Leslie Harrison Papers on the Federal Reserve System. Harrison was a deputy governor (1920-28), the governor (1928-36), and president (1936-41) of the Federal Reserve Bank of New York. Harrison's personal files, covering the period of his association with the Bank (1920-40), contain many official memoranda and other documents. Items are identified by the titles of sections of the Papers, as follows: Conversations, 1926-40 (cited as Harrison, Conversations); Office Memoranda, 1921-40 (Harrison, Office), both records of conversations, with some duplication; Miscellaneous Letters and Reports, 1920-40 (Harrison, Miscellaneous), copies of correspondence with the Federal Reserve Board and others; Open Market Investment Committee, 1928-40 (Harrison, Open Market), minutes of regular meetings, meetings of the executive committee, memoranda, correspondence, resolutions; Governors Conference, 1921-40 (Harrison, Governors), detailed agenda for meetings; Discussion Notes, 1930-40 (Harrison, Notes), minutes of meetings of the board of directors of the Federal Reserve Bank of New York and of the executive committee; Special Memoranda, 1933-40 (Harrison, Special), discussions of policy questions prepared by the Bank's research staff.

SOURCES OF CHARTS

CHART 16: Simon Kuznets, *Capital in the American Economy*, Princeton for NBER, 1961 (from worksheets underlying the book, variant III, component method, money income and real income). Money income divided by real income (implicit price deflator). *A Monetary History*, Table A-1, pp. 708-713, col. 8 (money stock); Table A-5, p. 774, col. 1 (velocity of money). *Historical Statistics of the United States, 1789-1945*, Bureau of the Census, 1949, p. 344 (wholesale price index). *Industrial Production, 1959 Revision*, Board of Governors of the Federal Reserve System, 1960, p. S-151 (industrial production). *The National Bureau's Research on Indicators of Cyclical Revivals and Recessions*, NBER, Dec. 1960, p. 5 (reference dates).

CHART 27: *A Monetary History*, Table A-1, pp. 712-713, cols. 1, 2, 3, 4, 8.

CHART 28: *Business Cycle Indicators*, G. H. Moore, ed., Princeton for NBER, 1961, Vol. II, p. 139 (personal income). *Historical Statistics of the United States, 1789-1945*, Bureau of the Census, 1949, p. 344 (wholesale price index). *Industrial Production, 1959 Revision*, Board of Governors of the Federal Reserve System, 1960, p. S-151 (industrial production).

CHART 29: *Common-Stock Indexes, 1871-1937*, Cowles Commission for Research in Economics, Bloomington, Ind., Principia Press, 1938, p. 67 (common stock price index). *Banking and Monetary Statistics*, Board of Governors of the Federal Reserve System, 1943, pp. 450-451 (commercial paper rate); pp. 469-470 (yield on corporate bonds, Baa, and on U.S. government bonds); p. 441 (discount rates).

CHART 30: *Federal Reserve Bulletin*, Sept. 1937, p. 909.

CHART 31: *A Monetary History*, Table A-1, pp. 712-713, col. 8, and Table B-3, pp. 803-804, cols. 1, 2, 3.

CHART 32: A. Liabilities. *A Monetary History*, Table B-3, pp. 803-804, col. 1 (high-powered money); Table A-2, pp. 739-740, col. 2 (bank deposits at Federal Reserve Banks); *Banking and Monetary Statistics*, pp. 411-412 (Federal Reserve notes, Treasury currency, gold coin and gold certificates), plus $287 million deducted by Federal Reserve added back to gold coin, seasonally adjusted by us.

B. Assets. *Ibid.*, p. 537 (monetary gold stock) plus $287 million deducted by Federal Reserve added back, seasonally adjusted by us; pp. 375-376, Federal Reserve credit outstanding and System holdings of U.S. government securities were each corrected for seasonal movements, and the latter subtracted from the former (Federal Reserve claims on the public and banks); high-powered money minus monetary gold stock minus Federal Reserve claims on the public and banks (other physical assets and fiat of the monetary authorities).

CHART 33: *Banking and Monetary Statistics*, pp. 375-376 (Federal Reserve credit outstanding; U.S. government securities held; bills discounted; bills bought), seasonally adjusted by us. "Other" obtained as a residual.

Author Index

Adams, Arthur B., 113
Anderson, Benjamin, 105, 108-109
Angell, James W., 114

Bagehot, Walter, 99
Beasley, Norman, 36
Bopp, Karl, 114
Burgess, W. Randolph, 80
Burns, Arthur F., 28
Burns, James M., 35

Chandler, Lester V., 75, 116, 117, 121-122
Chapman, John M., 29, 109

Fisher, Irving, 114, 117
Freidel, Frank B., 36
Friedman, Milton, 7

Galbraith, J. Kenneth, 11
Goldenweiser, Emanuel A., 81, 101-102, 104, 105, 109, 117, 134
Goldsmith, Raymond W., 59
Gordon, Robert A., 11
Graham, Frank D., 66

Hamlin, Charles S., 45, 68, 70, 71, 73, 80, 84-85, 102, 105, 118-119, 121-122, 134
Hammond, Bray, 33, 60

Hansen, Alvin H., 10, 113
Harrison, George L., 16, 21-22, 24, 31, 35, 43, 45, 47-48, 52, 54, 59-63, 65, 67-78, 80-95, 100-102, 105, 106-108, 110, 111, 116, 119, 121, 134
Hoover, Herbert, 18, 24, 29, 32, 35, 108

James, F. Cyril, 16
Jones, Jesse H., 29

Kemmerer, Edwin W., 115
King, Wilfred I., 114

Macesich, George, 4
Mitchell, Wesley C., 28
Reed, Harold L., 45, 114
Rogers, James H., 114

Salter, Arthur, 66
Schlesinger, Arthur M., Jr., 35
Schumpeter, Joseph A., 11
Smith, Rixey, 36
Sprague, Oliver M. W., 34, 115, 122

Thorp, Willard L., 33

Villard, Henry H., 108

Warburg, Paul M., 25
Warburton, Clark, 5, 32, 63, 110, 112
Willis, H. Parker, 29, 109, 115

137

Subject Index

(Page numbers in *italics* refer to tables and charts)

prices, decline in, 1931-32, 60
yields on, *8*, 16, 19, 23, 27-28
Great Britain:
cyclical trough of 1932, 19n
international credits to, 1931, 18
monetary policy of, 1931-32, 19n
Great Contraction, 1929-33, *see* Business contractions
Growth rate, computation of, 131

Hamlin, Charles, 12in
favored rise in discount rates. Oct. 1931, 85n
Harrison, George L., 122
Bank of U.S., attempt to save, 13n
easy money conditions denied by, Apr. 1931, 82
efforts to conciliate System, 73, 78, 81, 90-92
exchange with Glass, 92n
and expansionary monetary policy, 73
favored:
earlier and larger reductions in discount rates, 1930, 45
expansionary action, 1930, 1931, 74, 82
nationwide bank holiday, 31
purchases, Jan. 1932, 87
rise in discount rates, Oct. 1931, 85-87
foreign developments, concern over, July 1931, 83
on free gold, 107n
French urged by him to withdraw short-term U.S. balances, 101n
and Jan. 1933 System portfolio, 93-94
limited influence on System, 73, 118
loans to buy gold, attitude toward, 54n
member bank borrowing, hesitation to encourage, 110n
N.Y. Bank's authority to purchase for own account:
conflict with Gov. Young over, 68
reasons for N.Y. purchases, Oct. 1929, 70

view of other governors on, 70-71
O.M.I.C. and O.M.P.C. compared, 73n
opposed:
gold sterilization, 1930-31, 82
purchases in 1932 without Chicago and Boston Banks' participation, 91
High-powered money:
actual and hypothetical changes, 97-98
adequate supply, need of, 1929-33, 112n
changes in, 37, *40-41*, 44, 46, 49
opposite in direction to money stock, 1930-33, 36
contribution of, to change in money, 38
decline in, 44, 51
defined, 132
during banking panic of 1933, 53
rate of change in, 38
rise in:
due to gold inflow, 48
inadequate to prevent bank failures, 60
smaller than currency drain, 1931-32, 50
gold inflows, 49
national bank note increase, 1932-33, 52
rise in discounts and other Reserve credit, 50
Hoover, Herbert, 82
debt moratorium, and. 18, 82

Income, national, 2, 132
money, changes in, 3, 5
personal, 7, 8
real:
changes in, 3, 5
lower in 1933 than in 1916, 5
per capita, 5
percentage decline, U.S. and Canada, 1929-33, 56
Independent Treasury System, 4
Inflation and gold outflow, 100-102, 111

149